Moon Books Duets

The Morrigan

&

Raven Goddess

This edition is a bind up of two books:

Pagan Portals – The Morrigan
First published by Moon Books 2014
Text copyright: Morgan Daimler 2014
ISBN: 978 1 78279 833 0 (Paperback)
ISBN: 978-1-78279-834-7 (e-book)

Pagan Portal – Raven Goddess
First published by Moon Books, 2020
Text copyright: Morgan Daimler 2019
ISBN: 978 1 78904 486 7 (Paperback)
ISBN: 978 1 78904 487 4 (e-book)

Moon Books Duets
The Morrigan

&

Raven Goddess

Morgan Daimler

MOON
BOOKS
London, UK
Washington, DC, USA

CollectiveInk

First published by Moon Books, 2024
Moon Books is an imprint of Collective Ink Ltd.,
Unit 11, Shepperton House, 89 Shepperton Road, London, N1 3DF
office@collectiveinkbooks.com
www.collectiveinkbooks.com
www.moon-books.net

For distributor details and how to order please visit the 'Ordering' section on our website.

ISBN: 978 1 80341 711 0
978 1 80341 839 1 (ebook)
Library of Congress Control Number: 2024935727

A CIP catalogue record for this book is available from the British Library.

Design: Lapiz Digital Services

UK: Printed and bound by TJ Books Limited, Padstow, Cornwall
Printed in North America by CPI GPS partners

MIX
Paper | Supporting
responsible forestry
FSC
www.fsc.org   FSC® C013056

We operate a distinctive and ethical publishing philosophy in all areas of our business, from our global network of authors to production and worldwide distribution.

INTRODUCTION

"Sid co nem,
Nem co doman,
Doman fo nim.
Peace to sky
Sky to earth
Earth beneath sky"
– the Morrigan's Peace Prophecy

The Morrigan has been in my life for many years although her presence, like the moon, waxes and wanes. I have been honored to serve as her priestess in ritual and to teach about her across various media, and even now that she has stepped back from life as my journey leads me in a different direction I have a great deal of love for her. This book – both the books found here – are my offering to her and to you and I hope that they help to bring a greater understanding of her to the world and a stronger sense of both her history and her future.

In June of 2014 I attended the first annual Morrigan's Call Retreat in the US, a weekend full of ritual, magic, and workshops with some amazing people. I left that weekend inspired to write something that didn't exist on the market at the time: a basic introduction to the Morrigan. There were, of course, already books out there about the Morrigan but they were invariably either dense academic works or else popular books with little substance that only added confusion to an already confusing topic. I wanted to offer something to people that would provide some clarity, would help a reader sort through the tangle of information out there about the Great Queen. So I went home and began to write what would be Pagan Portals The Morrigan, trying to include what I felt was the most important information to people to know as they began their journey with this goddess or, for those already familiar, what seemed to be the most important information to sort through existing confusions. I went to source material directly and worked through the academic texts, but I also offered my own thoughts and experiences in little snippets after each chapter. I wanted to show that the Morrigan is a goddess rooted in Irish myth and history but also one who is active today.

When I wrote that Pagan Portal I intended it to be exactly what it is, a solid introduction, but I did always keep in the back of my mind the idea of someday following that introduction up with something that could dig deeper into some of the most common confusions and misinformation out there. The Morrigan is a wonderfully nuanced and hugely complex deity who takes time to get to know. Two years after writing that book I went to Ireland on a life changing tour of the Morrigan's sacred sites and my resolve to write more about her grew, although the time didn't feel right to do so. I knew I had more to say and that there was still a need for a specific type of Morrigan book, something short but aimed at untangling the most confusing aspects of her stories, but the idea for it hadn't fully gelled. The time wasn't right yet. It would be several more years, a total of five years after Pagan Portals the Morrigan, that things aligned for me to write Raven Goddess, tackling both the most common misunderstandings I saw around the Morrigan as well as offering a more in-depth look at her stories and associations. If Pagan Portals the Morrigan was an introduction to the goddess then Raven Goddess was the next step on that path, a way to get to know Herself beyond the basics. Even the name of the book was a nod to a more obscure detail of the Morrigan's mythology, a reference in the Sanas Cormaic to the Morrigan, Macha, and Badb as raven women which connected her to corvids outside the commonly imagined hooded crows.

I always intended the two books to work together and I wrote Raven Goddess to complement The Morrigan, so that readers could feel as if they were continuing a journey begun with the first book. Seeing these two texts together in this collector's edition is, for me, ideal as it allows them to fully work together as I'd always meant them to. They can now be read as a single book or taken in parts as needed and I truly hope that readers see the value of this. There are other, longer books on the Morrigan out there which have a lot of value but this is still, as far as I'm aware, the only introductory book that aims to help people get to know this goddess in an approachable way and to cut through the layers of misunderstanding that surround her.

The Morrigan moves still in the world today, in shadow and dream and in the hearts of those who seek her. May this book guide you on her path.

Morgan Daimler
Samhain 2023

About the Author

Morgan Daimler is a witch who has been a polytheist since the early '90's. Following a path inspired by the Irish Fairy Faith blended with neopagan witchcraft. Morgan teaches classes on Irish myth and magical practices, fairies, and related subjects in the United States and internationally. Morgan has been published in multiple anthologies as well as in Witches and Pagans magazine, and Pagan Dawn magazine, and she is one of the world's foremost experts on all things Fairy. Besides the titles available through Moon Books, Morgan has self-published a number of fiction titles, and has an urban fantasy/paranormal romance series called *Between the Worlds*.

MOON BOOKS

Pagan Portals (Celtic)
Lugh
Brigid
Aos Sidhe
The Dagda
The Morrigan
Irish Paganism
Raven Goddess
Manannán mac Lir
Gods and Goddesses of Ireland

Pagan Portals (Fairy)
Living Fairy
Fairy Queens
Fairy Witchcraft
21st Century Fairy

Pagan Portals (Norse)
Odin
Thor
Freya

Other Moon Books
Pantheon – The Norse
Travelling the Fairy Path
A New Dictionary of Fairies
Fairies A Guide to the Celtic Fair Folk
Fairy – The Otherworld by Many Names
Fairycraft – Following the Path of Fairy Witchcraft
Where the Hawthorn Grows – An American Druid's reflections

PAGAN PORTALS

THE
MORRIGAN

Meeting the Great Queens

MORGAN DAIMLER

Pagan Portals

The Morrigan

Meeting the Great Queens

Morgan Daimler

What People Are Saying About

The Morrigan

Morgan presents us with solid, well researched information on the Irish Morrigans from some of the best academic sources out there, and does it in a way that is engaging and approachable.
Segomâros Widugeni, previously known as **Aedh Rua**, author of *Celtic Flame: An Insider's Guide to Irish Pagan Tradition*

Pagan Portals: The Morrigan, is a well-researched and heartfelt guide to the Morrigan from a fellow devotee and priestess. Morgan Daimler's impeccable scholarship and devotion to the Morrigan offers readers both sound historical resources as well as the author's personal experiences with this complex goddess. A perfect guide for those taking the first steps towards understanding the Morrigan.
Stephanie Woodfield, author of *Celtic Lore and Spellcraft of the Dark Goddess*

There are so many faces of this amazing goddess and Daimler brings them together in a very readable way that enchanted me into turning page after page.
Elen Sentier, author of *Elen of the Ways* and *Trees of the Goddess*

For those who seek the Morrigan and related goddesses, Morgan Daimler's short book packs a lot of information into a small space. Balancing historical information with modern insights and practices, it is an excellent text for new seekers and devotees. Each section of the book contains both the results of her reading and short discussions of her personal experience, giving it a valuable and much-needed balance between research and practice. I particularly enjoyed the section on her insights about reconstructing seership practices with the goddess Badb. **Erynn Rowan Laurie**, author of *A Circle of Stones and Ogam: Weaving Words of Wisdom*; co-author of the CR FAQs

CONTENTS

Dedicated to Macha, the Goddess I serve – may I always serve you well.

I'd like to thank everyone who inspired this book, especially the wonderful people of Morrigu's Daughters (and Sons). To Stephanie, Mayra, and Natalie, for helping me see the joy in service, and to Ivy and Melody, the Pine Cabin Crew, for letting me see the Morrigan through new eyes. To Ed, Michelle, Gina, Dawn, Jenna, and everyone else at the Morrigan's Call retreat. To Maya for constructive criticism and Allison for helpful suggestions. And to my three children, Grayson, Aries, and Terence for supporting my writing and inspiring me.

This book is for everyone who seeks the Morrigan and doesn't know where to start.

Author's Note

There are many very good books out there on the Morrigan, most of which are academic and some of which are very hard to find due to cost or age. People who are just finding themselves drawn to this increasingly popular but often enigmatic Goddess are left with a quandary; long, in-depth books which may be hard to get through on one hand, and a sea of questionable internet resources which are short and easier but often untrustworthy on the other. This book was written as a resource for seekers that will offer both solid academic material and anecdotes of connecting with the Morrigan in a format that is accessible and designed to be easy to read. It is meant to be a basic introduction to this Goddess and several closely related Goddesses by the same name, and also a bridge for beginners to feel more comfortable with the longer, more scholarly texts.

In writing this I have drawn on many different sources and have carefully referenced and cited all of them. My own degree is in psychology so I prefer to use the APA method of citations. This means that within the text after quotes or paraphrased material the reader will see a set of parentheses containing the author's last name and date the source was published; this can then be cross references with the bibliography at the end of the book. I find this method to be a good one and I prefer it over footnotes or other methods of citation, which is why it's the one I use.

While this book can and does serve as a stand-alone work, ideally, I hope that the reader will be drawn to learn more and decide to continue seeking. To help with this I have provided a list of both the references I used in my writing and also of recommended further reading at the end of the book under the bibliography. I have tried to offer books which represent an array of options for people with different viewpoints and approaches to honoring the Morrigan.

I do not think ultimately the framework we choose to use for our religion matters as much as that we make the effort to honor the old Gods and bring their worship into the modern world in ways that respect their history. I don't think a person has to follow a specific religion, be it Reconstructionist, Wiccan, or Celtic pagan, to do this if they are coming to the Gods with a sincere heart and good intent. To that end this book is written without any specific spiritual faith in mind, beyond polytheism, and it is up to the reader to decide how best to incorporate the material. However, my own religious path is Irish Reconstructionist polytheism and so that is bound to color some of my opinions in the text.

I have been an Irish pagan since 1991 and actively honoring the Morrigan since around 2000; I am a priestess of the Goddess Macha, often named as one of the Morrigans. I can say with certainty that her path isn't an easy one and it is one that will always push a person to keep learning and moving forward. In each chapter I am going to include a little section on my own personal experiences with the Morrigan, because I want to help people see that she is an active force in the world today and how we can honor her, beyond the bounds of any one faith. For some people this book may be the first step in a life-long journey. For others, perhaps, she doesn't call to you in that way, but nonetheless something valuable can be gained here, if only a greater understanding of the Goddess, her history, and modern beliefs and practices associated with her.

Introduction

The Morrigan was an important figure in Irish mythology and she is active still in the world today. She reaches out to us from the pages of the old myths, in the stories of the traditional storytellers, and in modern songs. She comes to us on shadowed wings, in the still darkness, and in flashes of dreams. We hear her voice in the pounding of our own pulse, in the cry of the raven, and in the wild wind. She is a powerful force, but one that is often difficult to understand for those seeking her.

When we first feel the Morrigan's call we are confronted by a dizzying array of books and online sources purporting to teach us who she was and is. It quickly becomes clear though that the truth about the Morrigan is not so easily uncovered. Modern approaches to this ancient Goddess are often divorced from historic evidence of her; in contrast the older material can be harder to find and difficult to understand. Some put too much emphasis on personal experience while others ignore it. Ideally a modern seeker should try to find balance between all of these extremes.

There are several immediate challenges to face when we try to study the Morrigan. The first is understanding what her name itself means; not an easy thing because there is no clear answer. Next, we have to understand that Morrigan is used as a name, a title, and a noun, so that we can find stories about the Morrigan – as well as the three Morrignae, or Morrigans, in English – about different named Goddesses being called Morrigan in certain contexts, and also about certain supernatural beings called morrigan. Seekers are also confronted with an array of traditional lore which is often contradictory and with concepts from ancient Ireland that have different meanings than we tend to think of, because they are coming from a different context, a different culture. All of these difficulties must be addressed at the very outset in order to move forward and learn about who the Morrigan was and to help understand her in a modern framework.

First let's look at the possible meanings of her name and see what each one can tell us about her character. The etymology of the name Morrigan is somewhat disputed, but the current leading theory is that it means, roughly, nightmare queen – often given as phantom queen – although others still prefer the once popular "great queen" interpretation. The difference comes in depending on whether the first part of the name is given a fada (an accent mark in Irish which changes the sound of the vowel) and spelled Mor or Mór. Generally, the accepted meaning of "Mor" is to relate it back to Old High German mara and Anglo-Saxon maere, meaning nightmare, although when accented, mór, it means great, large (eDIL, n.d.). Some people also try to relate mor to sea or ocean, thus rendering her name as meaning sea queen and tying her to the Morgan la Fey of Arthurian legend, but this is not widely accepted (eDIL, n.d.). Another theory is that mor relates to the Indo-European word móros, meaning death, and that the name means queen of the dead or queen of the slain (Gulermovich Epstein, 1998). The second part, rígan or rigan means queen or noble lady (eDIL, n.d.). Unfortunately, there is no certainty on what the original meaning was. We can say though that the old Irish seems to have always been spelled Morrigan and likely did use the older meaning of nightmare queen, while the Mórrígan spelling was seen in the Middle Irish period along with the "great queen" interpretation. Looking at all of these together we see that her name could mean queen of phantoms, great queen, sea queen, or queen of the slain and each of these may hint at who she is and what she does.

The name is applied not only to a specific singular Goddess, but also to that deity's sisters, Badb and Macha. The Goddesses Fea and Nemain are also sometimes called Morrigan, and can be interchanged with the previous named Morrigan to form the different Morrigan triplicities. Personally, I favor viewing the three Morrigans as Badb, Macha, and Morrigu and I am willing to accept Anand as the name of the Morrigan (this will be discussed in depth in the next chapter). It can be difficult at times to know whether we are talking about the individual Goddess who more often uses the title as her name or whether we are talking about a Goddess being given the title Morrigan. Sometimes context can be helpful here, but other times we can only guess and even the scholars don't agree in every situation. To complicate the issue further the word morrigan is used as a gloss, or translation, of the Greek word lamia and also is used in the same way for the word specters in some sources (Gulermovich Epstein, 1998). This means that when we look at the older material it is always best to be cautious when seeing the name Morrigan until context is understood.

Another problem that must be dealt with in studying the historic material relating to the Morrigan is that the old texts are often contradictory and include variations in the stories which can be significantly different. There are rarely single cohesive versions of any story, rather each one will have multiple versions, sometimes called redactions, which may have very different details. This means that what can seem a certainty in one version may be non-existent or contradicted in another. No single text should ever be read as if it were the authoritative version, but rather multiple redactions have to be read and then decisions made on the likeliest agreement of the information, that is what to be believed and what to be set aside. Nothing in Irish mythology or folklore is simple or straightforward, from genealogies to plot details, and often the deeper we look the muddier the picture becomes.

Finally, a thoroughly modern problem of the Morrigan as an ancient Irish war Goddess is simply that we, as modern people, often don't understand what war was to the early Irish and hence what exactly a war Goddess was to them. Our modern wars are a far, far cry from the ancient battles and our society is structured in entirely different ways. While war has been and will always be a bloody, dangerous affair, war to the early Irish often revolved around cattle raids and involved small groups rather than huge armies as we would understand that concept today. Battle was done in a strictly honorable way, in equal combat, often one on one or with matched armies, and we see this emphasized repeatedly in the old stories. Gulermovich Epstein in her dissertation *War Goddess: The Morrigan and her Germano-Celtic Counterparts* describes Irish martial practices as including: prediction of battle, incitement of the warriors, loud noise, direct attack, rejoicing in bloodshed, and declaring victory (Gulermovich Epstein, 1998). All of these are features common to the Morrigan when she is involved in warfare and demonstrate how she in many ways embodied the Irish practices of warcraft. The Morrigan is indeed a war Goddess, but her wars are played out in hand to hand – or more aptly sword to sword – combat, in the skill of a fighter against an opponent, in the cleverness of the cattle raid, in courage and skill and the will to win.

Understanding the Morrigan is a process. It involves understanding the individual Goddesses called Morrigan as much as understanding the Morrigu herself. It means understanding her different roles in mythology and the importance of the forms she can assume. And it means understanding how all of the historical material ties in to modern worship and shapes her place in the modern world.

Chapter One

Morrigu – Goddess of Battle

Badb and Macha, greatness of wealth, Morrigu
springs of craftiness,
sources of bitter fighting
were the three daughters of Ernmas.
(Macalister, 1941)

The name Morrigan is a title, but is also used as a personal
name usually prefaced by "the". It appears in various forms
including Morrigu, Morrigna, and Morrighan; the modern Irish
is Mórríoghain. When all three of the Goddesses who share the
title Morrigan are being referred to together you will see it as
Morrignae, although for the purpose of this work I will gloss
that as Morrigans.

Historic Material
In the Lebor Gabala Erenn we are told: "*Delbaeth ... has three
daughters, the famous war-furies Badb, Macha, and Morrigu, the
latter sometimes called Anand or Danand.*" (Macalister, 1941). She
is the daughter of Ernmas according to the same text: "*Ernmas
had other daughters, Badb, and Macha, and Morrigu, whose name was
Anand.*" (Macalister, 1941). Her mother, Ernmas, is called both a
farmer and a sorceress of the Tuatha De Danann and her father,
Delbaeth, is one of the kings of the Gods. This potentially ties
her into different aspects of sovereignty and magic through her
parentage. We also know from this that her two sisters are Badb
and Macha, themselves also called Morrigan in different places,
and all three together are called an trí Morrignae, the three
Morrigans. She has three other sisters as well, Banba, Fotla, and
Eriu, the three sovereignty Goddesses of Ireland.

The material from the Lebor Gabala Erenn tells us that the Morrigan's name could actually be Anand or Danand (or Anu or Danu1) and indeed both are given as her name in various portions of the text (Macalister, 1941). For example, in verse 62, she is listed as one of the sisters with Badb and Macha: *"Badb and Macha and Anand, of whom are the Paps of Anu in Luachar, were the three daughters of Ernmas the she-farmer."* (Macalister, 1941). When the Anu connection is accepted some people further relate her to Aine who we will discuss in a later chapter (Berresford Ellis, 1987; Jones, 2009). The connection to Danu is based on the idea that Anu and Danu are the same Goddess; this would make her the ultimate progenitor or matriarch of the Tuatha Dé Danann. A single portion of the Lebor Gabala Erenn says: *"The Morrigu, daughter of Delbaeth, was the mother of the other sons of Delbaeth, Brian, Iucharba, and Iuchair: and it is from her additional name 'Danann' the Paps of Ana in Luachair are called, as well as the Tuatha De Danann."* (Macalister, 1941).

However, it should be noted that in multiple sources including the Cath Maige Tuired, Morrigan and Danand are listed separately; making it unlikely that Danu or Danand is one of the Morrigans. Indeed, Danand is the daughter of the Goddess Flidais according to one version of the LeBór Gabala Erenn, not a child of Ernmas (Macalister, 1941). The evidence for Anu or Anand is stronger and more persuasive, but Anu herself is an obscure Goddess; the Sanas Cormaic says that she, Anand, is the mother of the Irish Gods (Jones, 2009). It is probable that Anand may be the name of the Morrigu, but I find the evidence connecting her to Danand much less solid. Part of the reason for this is that the names Anand and Danand have different meanings, "abundance" and "flowing" respectively, which make it seem far more likely that the two were separate Goddesses later conflated due to the similarity in their names. It is also likely, in my opinion, that some of the variations and confusion reflect different regional beliefs later fused together when the stories were written down.

Relationships

Morrigu is sometimes said to be the wife of the Dagda. In the Book of Lecan we are told: *"Anand .i. in Morrigan… bean aile do'n Dagda,"* meaning: "Anand, that is the Morrigan… is the wife of the Dagda" (Heijda, 2007). She is said to have had a daughter, Adair, by the Dagda, and 26 daughters and 26 sons who were all warriors by an unnamed father or fathers (Gray, 1983; Gulermovich Epstein, 1998). In fairness to different viewpoints some people do interpret these 52 warriors not as physical children but as people dedicated to her.

Possibly her most well-known child is her son, Meche, by an unnamed father. Meche had three serpents in his heart, which could have destroyed all of Ireland, so he was killed and his heart burned; the ashes were put in a river where they killed all the animal life (Gray, 1983). According to the invasion myths she had three sons, Glon, Gaim, and Coscar, by an unknown father and three other sons, Brian, Iucharba, and Iuchair, by her own father Delbaeth (Macalister, 1941).

Forms

The Morrigan has many forms. She often appears as a crow or raven and is well known for taking this shape. In the Táin Bó Cúailgne, and possibly the story of Da Derga's Hostel, she appears as a heifer, and in many myths, she is associated with stealing cattle. She can be a beautiful young woman or a terrifying old hag, a bird, a wolf, an eel, or a cow. She appears in the air, on land, and in the water. Unlike many other Irish deities, she is explicitly referred to as a Goddess at least twice in the historic material and we have one ancient prayer to her. In the prayer she is being called on by a man who says she had previously been good to him and is asking for her help in gaining a herd of cattle (Gulermovich Epstein, 1998).

Associations

The Morrigan is a Goddess with many skills and powers. She appears to both the Dagda and to Cu Chulainn offering victory if they have sex with her; one agrees and one refuses. In the Táin Bó Cúailgne, Cu Chulainn spurns her amorous advances and she sets herself against him; the two fight and he deals her three wounds, which she later tricks him into healing. In the Cath Maige Tuired, she unites with the Dagda and after lying with him promises to fight alongside the Tuatha Dé Danann in the coming battle.

In mythology, the Morrigan aids the Tuatha Dé Danann in fighting against both the Fir Bolg and the Fomorians by using magic to shower fire, blood and fog upon the enemy and to weaken or kill one of the opposing kings (Gray, 1983; O hOgain, 2006). Indeed, in these battles she uses both magic and physical battle to defeat the enemy of the Tuatha Dé Danann. The second battle of Maige Tuired lists the three Morrigans as Druids, and the Banshenchas lists them as witches (Gray, 1983; Banshenchas, n.d.). She appeared before the battle of Mag Rath as a thin, grayhaired old woman who flew over the battlefield and leapt from spear point to shield rim of the soldiers who would win the battle during the fight (Smyth, 1988).

The Morrigan is associated with war, battle, and death, certainly, but also with victory, strategy, magic, and possibly sovereignty. She can give courage or take it away. She is a Goddess of glory in battle and the cleverness of the cattle raid, which was an essential aspect of early Irish society. Several authors posit that her connection to cattle relates to her role as a sovereignty Goddess. O hOgain goes the furthest in suggesting she is a land Goddess and a mother Goddess through her possible connection to Danu (O hOgain, 2006).

Although it is unlikely that she is a mother Goddess by even a loose definition of the term she does seem to have sovereignty qualities as a Goddess who influences battles and therefore decides the outcomes of wars and kingship disputes. She often appears near or in connection with rivers, which might support the idea of her as a Goddess connected to water, and her association with the Paps of Anu, breast-shaped hills in County Kerry, and other locations may support her connection as a land Goddess. I tend to reject that association myself, but leave it up to the reader to decide for themselves based on the evidence. Her strongest associations are clearly with warfare and also with fate so that some people have connected her to the Norse Valkyries (Jones, 2009; Gulermovich Epstein, 1998).

Several locations are named for the Morrigan including the whirlpool of Corryveckan, which is sometimes called the Morrigan's Cauldron. The river ford known as the "Bed of the Couple" is named for her Samhain tryst with the Dagda. Gort na Morrigna, field of the Morrigan, in county Louth is hers as is Fulacht na Morrigna, Morrigan's Hearth, in county Tipperary (Smyth, 1988). In the Bóyne valley Mur na Morrigna, mound of the Morrigan, is also hers as well as Da Chich na Morrigna, the Paps of the Morrigan (Smyth, 1988; O hOgain, 2006). The cave of Cruachan, also called Uaimh na gCait or Oweynagat (cave of cats), is especially associated with her and is the site of another of her cattle stealing episodes.

Poem for the Morrigan
She is blood and battle and death
The blade that cleaves flesh from bone
That cuts the old from the new
That reshapes, remakes, redefines us
Blood is not to be feared; it is the current of life
Battle is not to be feared; it is the price of sovereignty

Death is not to be feared; it is the end of the old...
And a new beginning, endlessly

An Offering Prayer to Anu
Great Battle Queen
Anu of the Tuatha De Danann
Called Morrigu
Who promises to deliver
Two handfuls of your enemy's blood
Who promises to catch what is chased
And kill what is captured
Mighty Anu of the people of skill
Accept this offering from me

Invocation to the Morrigan
Queen of battle,
Queen of war
Shape-shifting woman
Raven, wolf, and heifer
Bathing in bloodshed
Offering life or death
Obscurity or glory
Strong shield and
sharp spear point
Morrigan
I call to you

The Morrigan in My Life

I believe the Morrigan respects physical and martial skill and so am seeking to honor her in those ways as best I can; as part of this I am working on training in self-defense and basic martial skills. I created a small shrine to her that includes images of her animal forms and have been meditating on what each one represents, as well as the connection between her and war, death, battle, victory, strategy, magic, and sovereignty. I think it is possible that Anand may be connected to some aspect of mothering, but I see her as the defensive and protective aspects of mothering not the nurturing ones; she is the snarling wolf willing to rip the throat out of anything to protect her puppies, just as Morrigu fought to protect the Tuatha De Danann from the Fir Bolg and Fomorians. As we can see from her stories, she is a Goddess who expects a price to be paid for her blessing; nothing with her is free or easy.

My experiences with the Morrigan under the name Anu have been interesting. I find her energy to be very deep and solid, reminiscent of a standing stone. There is an immensity to her that is hard to describe, but decidedly numinous to experience. I see her as an intense younger woman with dark hair and a slim form, but to me she also had an oddly hooded or shadowed appearance, as if what I was seeing wasn't entirely set or decided.

Chapter Two

Macha – Goddess of Sovereignty

Macha: an tres morrīgan, unde mesrad Macha .i. cenda doine iarna n-airlech.

Macha: the third Morrigan; Macha's crop: the heads of slaughtered men
O'Mulconry's Glossary, 8th century (Jones, 2008)

Macha's name is connected to crows, cattle, pastures and fields. It's possible that her name may mean plain or field (Sjoedstedt, 2000). The electronic dictionary of the Irish language lists several meanings for the word in Old Irish including Royston (hooded) crow, milking yard/field, and field or plain. In modern Irish the word means cattle field or yard, a fine group of cattle in a pasture, or, when added to brea bó, a herd (O Donaill, 1977).

Historic Material

Macha is one of the Tuatha Dé Danann who appears in several different places in Irish mythology. She is a daughter of Ernmas, sister to Badb and Anand; these three sisters make up the triple Morrigan. In some sources Macha herself is called Morrigan; specifically in the Book of Femroy Macha is given as another name for the Morrigan, "*Macha .i. in Morrigan*", Macha, that is, the Morrigan (O hOgain, 2006; Heijda, 2007).

Macha is also referred to as Badb, given the name as a title in the same way she is called Morrigan (Coe, 1995). Although some people feel that only the Macha of the Tuatha Dé Danann is the Macha who is of the Morrigan others, myself included, feel that she appears several times in myth under the same name, but in different roles. There are also those who will argue that Macha herself is not the Morrigan at all, but a related deity with some overlapping functions. This chapter will present information on all the appearances of Macha and as usual leave it up to the reader to draw conclusions.

Macha appears in different guises in Irish mythology: as one of the daughters of Partholon, as one of the Nemedians, as one of the Tuatha Dé Danann, as a "fairy woman" and as a queen. This last one may or may not represent a pseudo-historic queen or a story about the Goddess. There is debate among modern followers of the Morrigan on this topic because the story has mythic overtones, but is not explicitly mythic, unlike her other appearances. However, many scholars do see Macha the queen as connected to the Goddess, as do I.

Macha Daughter of Partholon

In the first appearance of Macha, she is listed in the Lebor Gabala Erenn as one of the daughters of Partholon. Nothing more is said about her and nothing is known about her from this story except that it can be assumed she dies with all her people during a plague. Interestingly, however, we should note that the meaning of the name Partholon might be son of the ocean and when we see Macha later in the story of Macha, the fairy woman she lists her lineage as coming from the son of the ocean (Jones, 2008). This could be sign of the continuity between the different Macha stories.

Macha of the Nemedians

In the second story she appears as the wife of Nemed, of the third race to settle Ireland, and is said to die clearing the plains of Ireland for farming (Macalister, 1941). In alternative versions her husband cleared the land and he named it for her after she died. It was also said she had a vision of the future Táin Bó Cúailgne and the destruction and carnage it would cause and died of a broken heart (Green, 1992). Because she died clearing the land for farming, she is associated with the earth and its produce. The connection of the meaning of her name to cows and milking as well as fields and pasture, I think, also supports the view of her as a land Goddess. Interestingly John Carey in his essay "Notes on the Irish War Goddess" describes this Macha as both a seeress and a war Goddess, or woman who practices war magic (Coe, 1995).

Macha of the Tuatha Dé Danann

She appears in the Lebor Gabala Erenn among the Tuatha Dé Danann where she is called a daughter of Ernmas (Macalister, 1941). Several modern authors including Berresford Ellis and Jones suggest she was the wife of Nuada Argatlamh, king of the Tuatha Dé Danann, himself a complex deity, probably because the two are paired in battle and death in the Cath Maige Tuired and Lebor Gabala Erenn. This has become a popular belief and it is one I personally embrace as well, although the reader may form their own opinion. There is some supposition that it was Macha as Morrigan who joined with the Dagda a year before the second battle of Maige Tuired (Berresford Ellis, 1987).

In the Lebor Gabala Erenn it says: *"Delbaeth ... has three daughters, the famous war-furies Badb, Macha, and Morrigu..."* (Macalister, 1941). In this appearance she is killed in the second battle of Maige Tuired, but Macalister in one section of his notes on the Lebor Gabala Erenn volume IV says that it is logical to believe that this Macha and the fairy woman Macha who curses the men of Ulster are in fact the same being. Macalister also posits that the Morrigan was not originally a triplicity, and that Macha joined an existing Badb/Anand pairing, because Macha had her own center of worship at Armagh and he believes the genealogies suggest an earlier tradition to which Macha was later added (Macalister, 1941).

This provides us a variety of interesting information about Macha. We learn that she is the daughter of Delbaeth and Ernmas, who we have previously discussed, and sister to Badb and Anand, and is one of the three Morrigans. We learn as well that her husband may be Nuada the king (twice) of the Gods and that she fights and dies with him in battle. We also learn through Macalister's commentary that it is likely that Macha originally had her own separate cult centered in Ulster, which over time merged with an existing cult of Badb and Morrigu to form the Morrigan triplicity we know today.

In the Cath Maige Tuired it is also hinted that she actually takes the battlefield, as she does in the Lebor Gabala Erenn, because it mentions her along with Badb and Morrigu accompanying the warriors to the battle. In the Banshenchas she is listed as one of the Tuatha Dé Danann's magic workers, listed either as witches or sorceresses. In the first battle of Mag Tuired, she acts with the other two Morrigans to use magic against the enemy by sending rain, fog, and showers of blood and fire upon the opposing army. The second battle of Mag Tuired lists the three Morrigans as ban-draoithe, or Druids (Gray, 1983). This tells us that not only is she a warrior but also a magic user, especially of battle magic, in support of the side she is on.

Macha the Fairy Woman

Next, she appears as a fairy woman in the prelude to the Táin Bó Cúailgne and marries a farmer or chieftain named Crunnuic (often given as Crunnchu); she appears in his home and acts the part of his wife without initially speaking a word to him, eventually becoming pregnant with twins. He goes to a festival held by the king who is boasting of the speed of his chariot horses. Crunnuic, despite being warned by Macha not to speak of her to anyone else, brags that his wife could outrace the king's horses, and the furious king demands that Crunnuic bring her immediately to race or forfeit his life. Macha is brought to the assembly, but begs for a delay as she is in labor. Despite her pleas she is denied her request and forced to race anyway. She wins, collapsing and birthing her twins just past the finish line, then curses the men of Ulster with nine days of labor pain in their greatest hour of need for nine times nine generations, before dying. In some versions of the story she doesn't die, but simply returns to the Otherworld, because Crunnuic broke her prohibition against speaking of her.

According to the Metrical Dindshenchas, Macha gives birth to a boy and girl named Fír and Fíal (Gwynn, 1924). Interestingly, possible meanings of the name Fír include true, a pledge, a test or an ordeal, and Fíal means faithfully, seemly, or decorous, so that Macha's two children could possibly have names meaning "true" and "faithfully". Although this is entirely speculative based on the word meanings in Old Irish, it does seem quite fitting given the story they appear in. Indeed, one translation of the Rennes Dindshenchas gives her children's names as Truth and Honor (Coe, 1995).

To this day the spot of the race and the twin's birth carries her name, Emain Macha, where for a long-time festivals and assemblies were held, especially at Lughnasa (McNeill, 1962). It is from this story that her associations with horses, childbirth, pregnancy, and, again, the produce of the earth – by marrying a farmer – are seen. There are several details that also connect her subtly to sovereignty as well; the horses she races are both white, a sacred color, and she herself is equated to the sun, land, and sea (Coe, 1995).

The Rennes Dindshenchas connects this Macha, Macha of the Nemedians, and the Macha of the Tuatha Dé Danann because all three are referenced in the same poetic entry. It is also important to note that the curse laid on the men of Ulster by this Macha is essential to the great Irish epic the Táin Bó Cúailgne, in which the Morrigan plays a significant role and which we will discuss in more depth in a later chapter.

Macha Mog Ruadh

In the final story we see her connection to sovereignty and battle. She is Macha Mog Ruadh, Macha Red-Hair; her father is one of three kings who rotate the kingship of Ireland every seven years. This Macha is listed as the 76th ruler of Ireland and said to have ruled around the 4th century BCE (Berresford Ellis, 1987). Her father dies and when his turn comes around Macha steps up to rule, but the other two kings refuse to co-rule with a woman.

Macha takes the battlefield and fights them, winning her right to rule, but when her seven years are up, she refuses to step down because she was ruling through victory in battle not by an agreement. One of her two rival kings dies and his five sons step up to challenge her, so she goes to them disguised as a leper and seduces each of them, binding them afterwards and forcing them in their defeat to build her fortress at Emain Macha.

Eventually she marries the final king, Cimbaeth, and they rule together. Although this story is often seen as pseudohistorical it has many mythic overtones, including the numbers of kings, years, and sons, as well as Macha going to the sons disguised as a leper. The Metrical Dindshenchas conflates this Macha with Macha the fairy woman and Macha daughter of Nemed (Jones, 2008). This supports the idea, at least, that historically there did not seem to be a clear, sharp division between the different Machas – instead they often seemed to have been seen as different manifestations of a single being.

Associations

Several authors suggest that Macha herself formed a triplicity historically, specifically Macha the Nemedian, Macha the queen, and Macha the fairy woman (Gulermovich Epstein, 1998; Coe, 1995). This idea in a modern context goes along with Dumezil's trifunctional hypothesis, which divided society into three segments, clergy, warriors, and producers, and related that to three functions: sovereignty, battle, and fertility. It is also argued that the three Morrigans fit this concept as well with Morrigu representing sovereignty, Badb battle, and Macha fertility. As with most things though, not everyone agrees with these ideas.

Traditionally the severed heads of enemy warriors were called "Macha's acorn crop" – another sign that she was a warrior Goddess (Sjoedstedt, 2000). The head was the seat of the soul in Irish belief, making the taking of heads particularly powerful. In the Táin Bó Cúailgne the hero Cu Chulainn's friend Fergus swears an oath saying: "*By the point of my sword, halidom3of Macha*" (O'Rahilly, 2001). This connects her again to warriors and establishes swords as something sacred to her, especially the point of the sword.

Macha is associated with Ulster, Armagh (Ard Macha) and Navan Fort (Emain Macha). She is often strongly associated with horses possibly because of the story where she races and wins against the king's horses; Cu Chulainn had a horse named Liath Macha, "grey of Macha", which wept tears of blood before Cu Chulainn's final battle and was described as the king of horses. We are told in the Lebor Gabala Erenn that the Liath Macha belonged to Macha herself (Macalister, 1941). This may be a reflection of her role as a sovereignty Goddess, with the horse as a symbol of the sovereignty (O hOgain, 2006). Horses and crows are animals often linked to her; in Cormac's glossary she is called "Macha the crow" (Green, 1992). Her name is also said to mean hooded crow in several different sources, not as a literal translation of her name, but that her name, like Badb's, was used as a name for the birds as well. In the Dindshenchas it is said that Macha's other name is Grian: *"Her two names, not seldom heard in the west, were bright Grian and pure Macha,"* and, *"...in the west she was Grian, the sun of womankind."* (Gwynn, 1924). The word Grian itself has multiple meanings, all relating to the sun; some meanings are given in the electronic dictionary of the Irish language as sun, shining, bright, radiant, and luminary. I wonder if this may be an attempt by the Dindshenchas to connect Macha and the fairy queen Grian of Cnoc Greine in county Limerick; if so it's a tenuous link as there are no other references to this or connecting Macha to the sun in any way. Grian is more often connected to Aine; however, we shall look at both in more depth in a later chapter.

Certainly, her position as a sovereignty Goddess is particularly interesting in light of her relationship with Nuada Argatlamh, king of the Tuatha Dé Danann. She is also a Goddess of battle and warriors, death, magic (especially battle magic), druidism, and prophecy. Green posits that Macha represents the sovereignty and fertility of Ireland and can be vengeful when the land or she herself is wronged (Green, 1992). O hOgain sees her as a mother-Goddess and Goddess of sovereignty and war, with a strong connection to horses as symbols of kingship (O hOgain, 2006). The majority of scholars also favor seeing her as a mother Goddess, Goddess of childbirth, and a horse Goddess, and many compare her to the continental Epona (Coe, 1995). Although of all the Morrigans she is the most overtly sovereignty oriented, one cannot downplay war and battle as her purviews. She accompanies the warriors into battle and fights with the warriors in the Cath Maige Tuired, dying with her husband at the hands of Balor the Fomorian. The severed heads of those defeated in battle are her harvest and the sword point is holy to her, called her halidom in the Táin Bó Cúailgne. She is a complex deity and should be approached as such.

Here is a quick thought on all her deaths and reappearances. My own belief is that in each story when she "dies" she is actually just returning to the Otherworld from whence she came, having accomplished what she intended in our world. I'm with MacCulloch on this one: *"Pagan Gods are mortal and immortal; their life is a perennial drama, which ever begins and ends, and is ever being renewed – a reflection of the life of nature itself."* (MacCulloch, 1918).

Prayers to Macha

The following is a prayer I wrote to Macha, for strength in difficult times, when I was struggling to stay strong as a parent caring for a chronically ill child:

Macha, warrior, queen, Goddess,
you were a mother too,
help me now to be strong
you ran against horses
while laboring and won;
let me find the strength to
endure my own race
Macha, help me be strong
Give me the courage
to keep running

An Invocation of Macha

I call to you, Red-haired Queen,
Lady of sovereignty
I call to you, Woman of the Sí,
Who runs swifter than any horse
I call to you, Warrior Goddess,
Who gathers heads as trophies,
Fertile plain, racing mare, battle crow,
Macha, be with me now.

A Prayer to Macha
Macha, Druidess of the Tuatha de Danann,
Skilled in magic, great in power, full in knowledge,
Guide my feet on my path, as I honor the old wisdom
Guide my hands in offering, as I honor the old Gods
Guide my heart in strength, as I honor the old ways.

Invocation to Macha
Great Goddess, Mighty Macha,
Clearer of plains
Speaker of prophecy
Lady of the Holy People
I call to you
Warrior and Druidess
Wielder of fierce magic
Queen of the Tuatha De
I call to you
Sun of womanhood
Swifter than steeds
Lady of the Sí
I call to you

Each verse above could be used as a stand-alone with the first line if preferred.

The Morrigan in My Life

I have found Macha to be fiercely loving and protective of those she calls her own, with a strong maternal energy to her, but she can be very no-nonsense and unbending as well. She always appears to me as a red-haired warrior woman wearing a cloak of black feathers and riding or walking next to a black or white horse, sometimes both. To me she is a Goddess of the sovereignty of the land, a protector of the weak, and Goddess of women and women's issues, especially pregnancy and childbirth. She is also battle and pride and the will to win, and her spirit is the warrior's spirit.

Because horse races were a common event at Lughnasa celebrations and because such celebrations were held at that time at her sacred places, especially Emain Macha, I tend to associate that holiday with her in particular. In one version of the Dindshenchas we are told that on Mag Macha, Macha's Plain, there were memorial fairs held for her, called Oenach Macha (Coe, 1995). These fairs and the reason for them are strongly reminiscent of Lughnasa as well and reinforce her probable connection to that holiday.

Chapter Three

Badb – Goddess of Prophecy

Delbaeth ... has three daughters, the famous war-furies
Badb, Macha, and Morrigu,
the latter sometimes called Anand or Danand.
(Macalister, 1941).

The name Badb is very difficult to define and its etymology is complicated and contested. Some sources trace it back to the root bodvo, which means crow, while others tie it in to buduo meaning battle; a third option relates it to bhedh, which means to stab or cut (Heijda, 2007). All of these possible root meanings have strong points and relate to different aspects of the Goddess Badb. The eDIL describes the word Badb as being both the name of a Goddess and meaning *"Scald-crow; deadly; fatal; dangerous; illfated; warlike; venomous"* (eDIL, n.d.).

Scald crow is another name for the hooded crow, or Caróg liath in Irish (corvus cornix), a type of crow that is predominantly gray with black wings and head, giving a hooded appearance. This crow is a form taken by the Morrigan and in particular by Badb. Badb is also spelled Badhbh or Bodb and may be pronounced Bayv or Bibe. I favor pronouncing it Bayv, which goes with the Badhbh spelling. She may also be called Badb Catha, or battle crow and some people suggest a connection between her and the Gaulish Cathbodua.

Historic Material

Badb is the daughter of Delbaeth and Ernmas, sister to Macha and Morrigu/Anann, and is said to have two children, Ferr Doman and Fiamain (Macalister, 1941; Gray, 1983). In the

19

Banshenchas she is said to be the wife of the Dagda. This might be why people sometimes identify her as the Morrigan who slept with the Dagda on Samhain, although as already discussed others suggest this may have been Macha. In other cases, she is said to be the wife of the battle God Net along with Nemain. Other possible husbands are found elsewhere: listed in the Banshenchas is Indui, who is Net's father, and in the Lebor na hUidre her husband is Tetra (Heijda, 2007).

In mythology Badb is described both as being the Morrigan and also being the Morrigan's sister. In some versions of the Táin Bó Cúailgne it is also said that it is Badb, not the Morrigan, who contests with Cu Chulainn in the form of an eel, wolf, and heifer, and in one version of the Táin Bó Regamna we see the same alternate where she is called Badb instead of Morrigan (Heijda, 2007).

Badb is sometimes identified as Bé Neit, often translated as the wife of Neit. However, Gray suggests this might actually be a title meaning "Goddess of battle" (Gray, 1983). This can seem very confusing on the surface, but it is clear that originally Badb was an individual Goddess in her own right and only later did she start to merge to some degree with her sister the Morrigan, and vice versa, in a way that caused confusion.

Forms

Badb can appear as a withered hag or as a seductive young woman, as well as taking the form of a crow (Smyth, 1988). She is often associated with the colors black and white in descriptions, the colors of hooded crows, but the red of fresh blood and gore is also connected to her. In many cases in the mythology, she is called the Red Badb or the red-mouthed Badb. She is also described as having a ghostlike appearance and being pale; after seeing her in a vision Medb calls her a "white lady" (Heijda, 2007).

Associations

She appears throughout the Táin Bó Cúailgne to incite Cu Chulainn to fight, and at the very end flies over him or perches on his shoulder signaling his death (Smyth, 1988; Green, 1992). Like the other Morrigans she is able to influence battle; her cries cause confusion, panic, and chaos (Green, 1992). In a battle of 870 CE, she was said to appear in great "din and tumult" and incite the armies to slaughter each other (O hOgain, 2006). At the battle of Clontarf in 1014 CE it is said that Badb appeared, screaming, over the battlefield (Berresford Ellis, 1987).

Badb is often linked to prophecy. In the Cath Maige Tuired, after the battle, it is said that: *"Then after the battle was won and the slaughter had been cleaned away, the Morrigan ... proceeded to announce the battle ... And that is the reason Badb still relates great deeds. 'Have you any news?' everyone asked her then."* (Gray, 1983). After this she proceeds to prophesy a time of peace followed by a time of trouble. In the Tale of Da Derga's Hostel she is an omen of death, and she also appears in other cases as a washer-at-theford, washing the clothes or armor of doomed warriors (Green, 1992). Badb is often associated with the washer-at-the-ford because she frequently appears in this form. Before Cu Chulainn goes to his final battle he sees Badb as a beautiful young woman washing bloody clothes and keening, and before a battle between Toirdhealbhach and a Norman army she appeared and predicted doom for the Normans, which came to pass (O hOgain, 2006).

A difficulty with Badb similar to what we see with Morrigan is that the name is also both a title and a word. While she appears, especially in the older invasion texts, as an individual being, Badb is also used as title which is applied to other Goddesses including Macha and Nemain. As with the Morrigan we see Badb appearing in the plural, badba, or "badbs" in English, to indicate a group of related beings or group of beings acting in a Badb-like manner (Heijda, 2007). Beyond this badb is used as a word that means both hooded crow and also can be used for a beansidhe or beannighe4 or to describe any supernatural woman. O'Connell's Glossary describes the word badb as meaning: "*A female fairy, phantom, a specter...*" (Gulermovich Epstein, 1998). This creates situations where it is very difficult, reading some of the texts, to know if they are referring to the Goddess Badb, a Goddess of a similar nature, a fairy, a human witch, or a crow. Adding a final layer to this the word is also used as an adjective to mean warlike, deadly or furious (Heijda, 2007).

Invocation to Badb
Badb, daughter of Ernmas
Hooded Crow of Battle
Sister of Macha and the Morrigan
I call to you
Wife of Net, God of Warfare
Bringer of Madness
Washer at the Ford
I call to you
Badb of the Tuatha De Danann
I call to you

Prayer to Badb for Answers
Badb, who sees what has not yet come to pass
Who spoke the great prophecy when the battle
Between the Tuatha De and the Fomorians ended
Who spoke of both great peace and an end to all
Help me now to see what I need to see
To find the answer to the question I have
Open the way for me to receive my answer

Prayer to Badb before Prophesying
Badb Goddess of prophecy
May I see the past and the future
May I know the Truth of what is
May I find what I seek, and speak it
Badb, open the way for me
To see, to know, to speak
To prophesy of what was and
What is, and what will be
Badb, Goddess of prophecy
May it be so

Invocation to Badb
Scald-crow who cries over
the seething battlefield
Who dances on sword points
and washes the clothes of
those doomed to die
Speaker of prophecy
Badb, I call to you

The Morrigan in My Life

Although Badb is strongly associated with battle and carnage, to me Badb is mostly a Goddess of prophecy and omens. I often pray to her before doing divination work, whether it's reading tarot cards or interpreting omens, and especially any divination work of an Irish nature such as imbas forosnai (see the chapter on the Morrigan in the Modern World).

I associate crows most strongly with her and her altar includes images of crows and a large black feather, symbolic of her in that form. I have also gone to Badb in times of crisis, especially emotional crisis, for strength. When I have encountered her in dreams or journey work, she has an almost detached quality to her and has repeatedly encouraged me to take the long view in situations – to see the forest instead of the trees – and not to obsess over minutiae. I see her as a thinner, pale woman of indeterminate age with tangled black hair, piercing black eyes, and usually accompanied by a crow or three.

Chapter Four

The Morrigan by Other Names

Nemain

Nemain, Danand, Badb and Macha, Morrigu who
brings victory,
impetuous and swift Etain, Be Chuilli of the north
country,
were thesorceresses of the Tuatha De. (Banshenchus, n.d.)

Nemain, also called Neman, Nemon, or Nemhain, is probably the other Goddess most often included as one of the three Morrigans. Her name possibly means venomous or frenzy (Berresford Ellis, 1987; Green, 1992). However, the etymology is highly speculative and uncertain. In many modern popular books, she can be found listed along with Badb and Macha as the three Morrigan, as if she were the Morrigu. Hennessey in his 1870 book *The Ancient Irish Goddess of War* seems to have been the first to say that the Morrigan triplicity consisted of Badb, Macha, and Nemain, something that has often been repeated since. The quote from the Banshenchus above, however, demonstrates the older view clearly did not see her as the Morrigu, although she might have born the title of Morrigan as did Badb. Indeed, in the stories where Nemain appears she is most often paired with Badb alone and seems to act as a battle Goddess in her own right, separate from the three Morrigans who we often see acting together elsewhere.

Nemain is said to be the daughter of Elcmar, the original owner of Brugh na Bóyne and possibly an alternate name of Nuada. She is the sister of Fea and wife of Neit, an obscure God of war, although the phrase Bé Neit, which is translated wife of Neit, can also mean woman of war or battle and appears elsewhere as a name in its own right. To add to the confusion on this issue some sources describe her as the wife of Nuada and conflate her with Macha, while others describe her as an aspect of Badb (Berresford Ellis, 1987; O hOgain, 2006). In one source she is called beautiful and described as a judge (Gulermovich Epstein, 1998). All descriptions of her mention battle and war.

Nemain is associated with battle frenzy and exciting or terrifying armies. Her name itself is sometimes translated in the old texts as a word meaning battle fury or frenzy, and like Badb can be used to mean witch (Heidja, 2007). In the Táin Bó Cúailgne she appears twice, once to terrify Medb's army at night, and a second time when Cu Chulainn cries out in fury Nemain appears and wreaks havoc among the opposing army, causing the men to kill each other in confusion and fear (Hennessey, 1870). In the Táin Bó Cúailgne, she raises such a terrifying cry that 100 warriors die at hearing it. As mentioned above the Banshenchas lists her as a magic worker among the Tuatha Dé Danann, and the Lebor Gabala Erenn describes her as *"Neman of ingenious versicles5"* (Banshenchus, n.d.; Macalister, 1941).

Her place among the Morrigans is somewhat uncertain. It is clear in the Invasion texts that she was seen as separate from the three daughters of Ernmas, Badb, Macha, and Morrigu, although in later mythological cycles she does often appear acting with Badb or associated with her. As Gulermovich Epstein says, *"What is not clear is whether Nemain was actually considered one of the morrigna by the medieval Irish literati since most of the evidence… is circumstantial. However, if [we use morrigan as a general term] it seems appropriate to include Nemain in that group."* (Gulermovich Epstein, 1998).

Prayer to Nemain
Nemain
Furious, frenzied,
Screaming in battle
Laying low strong warriors
Nemain
Wife of War
Beautiful judge
Who knows no fear
Nemain
Help me find strength
Help me overcome fear
Help me be true to myself

Fea

Fea and Neman, the two wives of Net son of Indiu, two Daughters of Elcmar of the Brug. (Macalister, 1941).

Her name may mean hateful, in fact Cormac's glossary goes so far as to define it as meaning all things hateful (Berresford Ellis, 1987; Heijda, 2007). Other authors, however, relate it to the Irish words fee and fé, which mean death and a measuring rod for the grave, and possibly back to the Latin *vae* meaning an exclamation of woe (Gulermovich Epstein, 1998). As with Nemain though the etymology is uncertain and Fea is an obscure Goddess who we know very little about. She is said to be a sister of Nemain; both are daughters of Elcmar and both are wives of Neit according to the Lebor Gabala Erenn. Both Fea and Nemain in some of the genealogies are the nieces of the three previously named Morrigans (Gulermovich Epstein, 1998).

Fea is obscure, but seems to have been most strongly associated with south Leinster, especially Mag Fea, the plain of Fea, which bears her name (Heijda, 2007). Interestingly, Fea also has an association with cattle, as does the Morrigan. In the Dindshenchas she is connected to two oxen, Fe and Men; the same passage describes her as "silent" and "beloved" (Gulermovich Epstein, 1998).

Bé Neit

Another obscure battle Goddess associated with the Morrigan is Bé Neit, whose name can be translated as either wife of Neit or woman of battle. In one version of the Táin Bó Cúailgne Badb and Nemain appear along with Bé Neit to harass the Connacht army at night. There is very little information on this Goddess, and indeed, Heijda in her dissertation "War Goddesses, Scald Crows, and Furies" suggests that the identification of Bé Neit as a separate being is a scribal error and should actually say *"Badb, who is the wife of Net, and Nemain"*, rather than listing them as three individuals. Other sources list Bé Neit as Nemain, while still others say she is the Morrigan (Gulermovich Epstein, 1998). In one text we find out that Bé Neit was believed to have power over the outcomes of battles, *"…upon which of them battlemourning Be Neit would establish her mighty power (and so gain them the victory)"* (Gulermovich Epstein, 1998). It is possible that Bé Neit was meant to be understood as meaning woman of battle and could be used to describe any of the war Goddesses, rather than being a proper name.

Áine – or Anu?

In some modern mythology Áine (pronounced Awn-yuh or Awnuh) is seen as an aspect of Anu or the Morrigan (Berresford Ellis, 1987). Lady Gregory, writing in 1904, stated that some people in Ireland believed that Áine "was the Morrigu herself" showing that there was an old folk belief connecting the two (Gregory, 1904). However, while Anu's name means abundant, Áine's name is related to shining and brightness indicating a basic difference in the two deities; they also have very little mythology in common or that could be seen as similar. Interestingly, Grian, who we will also discuss, is seen as a possible aspect of Macha, probably due to a reference to Macha in the Metrical Dindshenchas that gives an epithet of Grian to her. While I disagree with these associations, I admit that I find it fascinating that Áine and Grian are strongly associated with each other and a possible division of the year, and each is also associated with the Morrigan and Macha respectively. I will give the reader what we know of Áine historically and leave it up to the reader to decide whether the connection to the Morrigan has any weight to it.

It's an interesting thing in Irish mythology and folklore that the Gods were reduced not into human characters, by and large, but into fairies. So, it is with Áine of Cnoc Áine in county Kerry, who is believed to have been a Goddess originally, but is held to be a Lady of the Sí now with the fairy hill of Knockainy being her special place. In Irish belief this is because after humans came to Ireland the Gods went into the sí, the hollow hills, and became the aos sí, the people of the fairy hills. This later evolved into seeing the Tuatha Dé Danann as part of the beings of Fairy, but because the modern – especially modern American – idea of what fairies are is so different from the traditional concepts this can cause confusion. The Gods are still the Gods, even in the sí, and it is a mistake to minimize them into twee little things because it's trendy to see fairies that way now. As to the idea of Gods as fairies my own view is that it doesn't really matter whether a being is a God in every story or sometimes appears as a fairy, as I see beings as on a scale of power where a powerful enough fairy and a God within a sí are effectively the same thing under different terms. It's sort of a po-tay-to/pah-tah-to situation where the label is incidental to the actual being.

Like most Irish deities, Áine has a complex and sometimes contradictory mythology. She is said in some sources to be the daughter of Manannan Mac Lir and in others to be the daughter of Manannan's foster son Eogabail, a Druid of the Tuatha Dé Danann (Berresford Ellis, 1987). No mother is listed for her. Some sources say that her sister is Finnen, whose name means white (Monaghan, 2004). Her name likely means brightness or splendor and she is often associated with the sun (O hOgain, 2006; Monaghan, 2004). In fact, not far from her hill of Cnoc Áine is another hill, Cnoc Gréine, associated with the Goddess Grian who is also reputed be a fairy queen; MacKillop suggests the two Goddesses might represent the summer and winter suns respectively and some sources list them as sisters (MacKillop, 1998; Monaghan, 2004).

In much of her later folklore Áine is reputed to have love affairs with mortals and several Irish families claim descent from her. The most well-known of these human descendants is the third Earl of Desmond, Gearoid Iarla. It is said by some that Gearoid did not die but was taken into Loch Guirr and would return one day (Berresford Ellis, 1987). Other tales say that he still lives within the lake and can be seen riding beneath the water on a white fairy horse, while still other stories claim that Áine turned him into a goose on the shore of the lake (Berresford Ellis, 1987). She was also said to have been raped by the king Aillil Olom, on Samhain, who stories say she either bit off an ear from, or she killed in punishment (Monaghan, 2004; Berresford Ellis, 1987; O hOgain, 2006). The child of this union was Eogan whose line went on to claim rulership of the land through their descent from the Goddess (Monaghan, 2004).

Áine is associated with fertility, agriculture, sovereignty, and the sun, as well as love (Berresford Ellis, 1987; Monaghan, 2004). She is especially connected to red mares, with some people claiming she could assume this form (MacKillop, 1998; Monaghan, 2004). She may also be associated more generally with horses and possibly with geese and sheep as they appear in her folklore. The hill of Cnoc Áine is one of the most well-known places connected with her, said to have been named after her during the settling of Ireland when she used magic to help her father win the area (O hOgain, 2006).

Midsummer was her special holy day and up until the 19th century people continued to celebrate her on the eve of midsummer with a procession around the hill, carrying torches of burning straw in honor of Áine na gClair, Áine of the Wisps (Berresford Ellis, 1987). Áine is also sometimes called Áine Chlair, a word that may relate to wisps or may be an old name for the Kerry or Limerick area (Monaghan, 2004; O hOgain, 2006). On midsummer clumps of straw would be lit on her hill and then scattered through the cultivated fields and among the cows to propitiate Áine's blessing (O hOgain, 2006). In county Louth there is a place called Dun Áine where people believe that the weekend after Lughnasa belongs to Áine, and in some folklore she is said to be the consort of Crom Cruach during the three days of Lughnasa (O hOgain, 2006; MacNeill, 1962). Additionally, there is another hill called Cnoc Áine in county Derry, and a third in Donegal (O hOgain, 2006). In Ulster there is a well called Tobar Áine that bears her name.

Whether a Goddess or fairy queen, Áine has been much loved, even up until fairly recently. Her mythology is convoluted but fascinating and any who feel the need or desire to honor a solar Goddess within an Irish framework would do well to learn more about Áine. As they say, she is "The best hearted woman who ever lived" (O hOgain, 2006).

Invocation to Áine
Queen of the sí of Cnoc Áine
Red mare who circles the lake
Lady of Midsummer bonfires
of straw torches and burning wisps
Áine of the harvest

Áine of the summer sun
Áine of the fairy hill
I call to you

Grian – Another Name for Macha?

Grian (roughly pronounced Gree-uhn) is an obscure Irish Goddess whose mythology is lost to us. She is not mentioned in any of the surviving stories or myths, except in brief references as Áine's sister. Grian appears in folklore as the queen of a sí, Cnoc Greine, as well as a lake, Loch Greine or Lough Graney, both in county Limerick (Berrisford Ellis, 1987; Smyth, 1988). Cnoc Greine is about seven miles from Knockainey, the sí of Áine (Smyth, 1988). In folklore Grian is said to be a sister of Áine and daughter of Fer I (Yew man), but little else is known about her family or relationships. Some authors including MacKillop and Smyth suggest that Grian may be an aspect of Áine, or another name for her, although I don't favor that idea myself.

The word grian, with a fada over the i, means sun, bright, radiant, sunny-faced, sunny, and meeting place; the word grian without the fada means sand, sea, river, base, foundation, earth, and land (eDIL, n.d.). Both meanings are intriguing to contemplate, although the generally accepted meanings connected to the name Grian relate to the sun. Grian is widely thought to be a sun or solar Goddess in a similar way to Áine. It may be possible that the connection to Áine is based on an older belief that Áine represented the strong summer sun, while Grian represented the more distant winter sun; in this way each sister would have been seen to rule over part of the year by controlling the sun during that time (MacKillop, 2008). With Áine's connection to midsummer celebrations it is possible that Grian would once have been honored at the winter solstice (MacKillop, 2008; Monaghan, 2004). This could be compared to the modern division of the year into a dark and light half at these times, and to the stories of the Oak and Holly Kings in neopaganism or the Scottish folk belief (also likely modern) of Brighid and the Cailleach sharing the year.

There may also be a connection between Grian and Macha that is worth considering as well. In the Metrical Dindshenchas it is said that Macha's other name is Grian: "...*her two names, not seldom heard in the west, were bright Grian and pure Macha*" and "...*in the west she was Grian, the sun of womankind.*" (Gwynn, 1924). Some suggest that Grian was used at times as an epithet and that this may be the case with Macha being called the sun of womankind (Monaghan, 2004). Unfortunately, there is nothing else referencing this connection in other sources outside the Dindshenchas that I am aware of, but taken with Áine's possible connection to the Morrigan it would not be unreasonable to accept.

While our information about Grian is scarce there is enough to give us a basic understanding of her as a Goddess connected to the sun who likely balanced the year with her sister Áine. Any association with Grian and the winter solstice is based on supposition, but that supposition is logical. Similarly, the connection of Áine and Grian to the Morrigan sisterhood, while more tenuous, could be used to better understand Grian through contemplating how she connects to or is an aspect of Macha.

Invocation to Grian
Queen of the sí of Cnoc Greine
Sister of Áine, daughter of Yew
Lady of the winter solstice
of cold, pale light shining on snow
Grian of the cold winds
Grian of the winter sun
Grian of the fairy hill
I call to you

Danu – Mother of the Gods

Danu is an obscure figure who appears only a handful of times in Irish mythology, and always under the genitive form of the name: "Danann" or "Danand". This has led many to suggest that the name of the Goddess is a reconstruction based on the name Tuatha Dé Danann, which is often translated as "people of the Goddess Danu". Tuatha Dé Danann itself is problematic as it may be a term added later by the Irish monks to differentiate the native Irish Gods from the biblical characters referred to as "Tuatha Dé" (People of God) in the writings, making the subject slightly more complicated.

Although many people assume Danann only shows up briefly in the Lebor Gabala Erenn, she does also make a couple appearances in the Cath Maige Tuired: "*The women, Badb, Macha, Morrigan and Danann offered to accompany them*" and "*...the three queens, Ere, Fotla and Banba, and the three sorceresses, Badb, Macha and Morrigan, with Bechuille and Danann their two foster-mothers*" (Gray, 1983). It is possible that the second reference is a transcription error and should read "Dinann", which would mean the list included Be Chuille and Dinann, the two daughters of Flidais listed as she-farmers in the Lebor Gabala Erenn, something that would make more sense in the context of the reference. However, the first appearance seems to stand alone. It's also worth noting that genealogies in the mythology are extremely convoluted between sources, so it is also possible based on the way that one redaction of the Lebor Gabala Erenn describes "Danand" as a daughter of Flidais, and later says it is Danu, not Flidais, who is Bechuille's mother, that the reference in the Cath Maige Tuired reflects a different understanding of the Goddesses. Danu is described as "mother of the Gods" and in some versions is equated to Anu, one of the Morrignae and a daughter of Ernmas (Macalister, 1941).

However, in different versions Anu is listed as the seventh daughter of Ernmas, making Danu/Anu a sister to the three Morrignae rather than one of their number. We see her equated to Morrigu and listed as the mother of three sons by her own father as well as mother of all the Gods, for example, here: *"The Morrigu, daughter of Delbaeth, was mother of the other sons of Delbaeth, Brian, Iucharba, and Iuchair: and it is from her additional name 'Danann' the Paps of Ana in Luachair are called, as well as the Tuatha De Danann."* (Macalister, 1941).

She is sometimes also equated to Brighid because both are listed in different places as the mother of the three sons of Tuireann. It is possible that Danu was a name used for Anu, the Morrigu or Brighid, but is also possible that the later references to Danu were added by monks seeking to give Danu more legitimacy as an important factor among the Gods. The third possibility, of course, is that there were originally regional variations of the stories that placed a different Goddess in the same role depending on which Goddess mattered in what region and the attempt to unify these stories created the muddy waters we have today.

Elsewhere in literature Danu is described as a Goddess and Druidess (O hOgain, 2006). She is sometimes called the mother of the Gods, but in other places is associated specifically with the three Gods of skill (O hOgain, 2006). It is extremely difficult to sort out any coherent list of her possible parentage, siblings, or children. Very little personal information is attributed to her that is not elsewhere applied to someone else, leading me to suspect that at least part of her story was grafted on at a later time.

Many modern authors associate her with the Welsh Don and with continental Celtic Goddesses based on the widespread use of the root word for her name Dánuv, which is associated, for example, with the Danube river. The name Danu itself seems to come from the Proto-Indo-European word for river6. She has associations with both rivers and as a Goddess of the earth; she likely was originally a river Goddess whose focus later shifted to the earth (O hOgain, 2006).

In modern myth we can find many new stories that include Danu; these are by nature based on the individual's personal inspiration. Alexei Kondratiev wrote an essay called "Danu and Bile: the primordial parents?" in which he links Danu and Bile as a likely pairing that could represent the parents of the Gods. Similarly, Berresford Ellis also sees Danu and Bile as a pairing. Some modern pagans and Druids have created elaborate creation stories involving these two and internet sources will list Danu as the mother of deities like Cernunnos and the Dagda. It is best to bear in mind the lack of substantial historic evidence relating to this Goddess and take much of the modern myth and information for what it is.

Creating a relationship with this Goddess would be challenging and would rely on personal intuition to a great degree. The lack of substantial information and mythology means we have only hints to work with. She is a river Goddess. She is a land Goddess. She is a mother of many children and a Druidess. Beyond this, let your own inspiration guide you.

The Morrigan in My Life

The Morrigan is a very complex Goddess, as are the other deities that are known under that title. Over the years as I have sought to deepen my knowledge of and connection to the three Morrigans I have also reached out to honor some of these other Goddesses who are so often connected to her. My own experiences have been mixed and I found some genuine connections and others that I did not resonate with at all.

My own personal experiences with Nemain are few. I have encountered her only a handful of times; she appears to me as a naked warrior, painted in the blood of her enemies. Her energy is fierce and terrifying even when she isn't trying to be. I have no personal experience with Fea or Be Neit, as such.

I have honored Aine on midsummer for many years, and am glad I do. My family bakes a cake for her every year, which we give as an offering to her and to the Fair Folk. I'm still not convinced she is one of the Morrigans, but I do think she is a powerful and complex Goddess.

I am only just building an understanding of Grian, but I am comfortable with associating her with the winter solstice and honor her on that day. I feel that she is the hope of growing warmth in winter, and of renewal; the promise of the solstice that the light of each coming day will be longer and that spring, no matter how distant, will arrive. I offer her spiced cider and sugar cookies, and as my family bakes a cake at midsummer for Aine, we dedicate the one we bake at midwinter to Grian.

Danu was actually the very first Irish Goddess I ever honored when I found Irish paganism. I see her in a very broad, all-encompassing way, as the mother of all. She appears to me as an immense woman dressed in green with dark hair and eyes. Her energy is like the earth, immeasurable and solid, and like the ocean, vast and yet with a feeling of movement to it. There is something indescribably old to Danu and an impersonal feeling to her as well.

Chapter Five

The Morrigan in Mythology

The Morrigan appears in a variety of different stories and myths in Ireland. Looking at these appearances and what the Morrigan does in each of them can be enormously helpful in trying to understand who the Morrigan was and is. It is beyond the scope of this work to make an exhaustive study of all of her stories, but I will try to offer the most significant for you to consider. It is also beyond this book to fully retell each story, so the focus will be on the portions featuring the different Morrigans. I strongly encourage people to read the full stories for themselves.

The Morrigan in the Invasion Myths

The Morrigan, Badb, and Macha appear in both the first and second Cath Maige Tuired stories. The first battle of Maige Tuired is the story of the Tuatha Dé Danann coming to Ireland and fighting for the land with the Fir Bólg – primordial beings who were already there. The second battle of Maige Tuired is the tale of the Tuatha Dé Danann fighting against the Fomorians, chthonic beings who they share Ireland with. In both stories the war Goddesses have important roles in defending their people.

In the first battle of Maige Tuired we initially see the three Morrigans when the battle with the Fir Bolg is about to be waged. We are told:

> *It was then that Badb and Macha and Morrigan went to the Knoll of*
> *the Taking of the Hostages, and to the Hill of Summoning of Hosts*
> *at Tara, and sent forth magic showers of sorcery and compact clouds*

of mist and a furious rain of fire, with a downpour of red blood from
the air on the warriors' heads; and they allowed the Fir Bolg neither
rest nor stay for three days and nights. (Fraser, 1915).

The magic of the three sisters is potent and the Fir Bolg are embarrassed that their own magic workers seem so powerless in contrast. Later, during the first round of combat the Fir Bolg poet, seeing the slaughter, declares that: *"The Red Badb will thank them for the battle-combats I look on."* (Fraser, 1915).

When the next battle occurs a list of the nobles of the Tuatha Dé Danann who go to the front to fight is given and with it we are told that Morrigan, Badb, Macha, and Danann accompanied them. Similarly on the fourth day of battle the three Morrigans, as well as their sisters the sovereignty Goddesses Eriu, Fotla, and Banba, and their foster-mothers Danann and Be Chuille, accompany the warriors. In this battle the Goddesses set up pillars behind their own army so that the warriors cannot retreat but must fight. Eventually the Tuatha Dé Danann triumph, although their king Nuada loses his arm during the fighting.

In the second battle of Maige Tuired the Morrigan appears to Lugh to urge him to rise up and fight against the Fomorians who are oppressing the Tuatha Dé Danann. It is this appearance which seems to set in motion the actual war between the two powers.

On Samhain the Morrigan met with the Dagda and they united before she promised to aid the Tuatha Dé Danann in the Cath Maige Tuired. We are told that a year before the battle the Dagda had arranged to meet the Morrigan near Samhain-time. He found her straddling a river, washing, with her hair hanging in nine sections. One foot was on the south shore and one on the north shore. He talked to her and they joined together, after which the site was called "The Bed of the Couple".

After having sex with him, the Morrigan tells the Dagda to gather the skilled Gods together and she will meet them near the river. She promises to go to one of the Fomorian kings, Indech, and to, *"...take from him the blood of his heart and the kidneys of his valor."* (Gray, 1983). When the hosts of the Tuatha Dé Danann meet up with her later she gives them two handfuls of blood as a symbol of her destruction of the king, and that place is called the "Ford of Destruction" afterwards. Although Indech is not killed then, he does die in the following battle, suggesting that her act may have been magical, with the blood representing her taking of his courage and strength, enabling him to be defeated in combat.

When the armies of the Tuatha Dé Danann have gathered and Lugh asks her what she will contribute to the fight she replies: *"'Not hard to say,'* ... *'I have stood fast; I shall pursue what was watched; I will be able to kill; I will be able to destroy those who might be subdued.'"* (Gray, 1983). In the battle itself we learn that Macha and Nuada both fall together at the hands of the Fomorian king Balor. Macha is the only female name listed in the recounting of the warriors who died in the battle and because of the context in which her name is given, it is entirely logical to assume she died fighting alongside her husband.

As to the Morrigan herself it was said: *"Then the Morrigu, daughter of Ernmass, came, and heartened the Tuatha De to fight the battle fiercely and fervently. Thereafter the battle became a rout, and the Fomorians were beaten back to the sea."* (Cross & Slover, 1936). After the victory of the Tuatha Dé Danann, Badb is asked to give the news and she recites a prophecy which tells of the fate of the world, both good and bad, to come.

The Morrigan in the Ulster Cycle

The main story of the Ulster cycle is the Táin Bó Cúailgne, the story of a war between two Irish provinces, Connacht and Ulster, over two great bulls who are actually enchanted cowherds that have assumed many shapes over different lifetimes. The primary characters of this Táin are the hero Cu Chulainn and the queen of Connacht, Medb, although the story is an epic which covers many years and includes a multitude of other minor characters, including Cu Chulainn's charioteer and Medb's husband. The Morrigan also plays a pivotal role as Macha, in a prequel to the main story, Badb, and Morrigu, and we see Nemain and Bé Neit as well.

No relationship in Irish mythology may be more complicated than that of the Morrigan and the epic hero Cu Chulainn. Some people feel that their relationship is an antagonistic one, with the Morrigan setting herself against him and ultimately causing his death; others feel that she loved him or otherwise favored him and her actions were designed to increase his glory as a warrior. My own opinion is in the middle – I think that the Morrigan engineered the events of the Táin Bó Cúailgne for her own reasons and she needed Cu Chulainn as part of it, but her relationship to him seems largely ambivalent. Her main focus seems to be on the war itself, and she is undeniably its cause. While she clearly favors Ulster, and for that matter the Brown Bull who she had bred to her own cow in the Táin Bó Regamna, she often seems to contend against Cu Chulainn and make his path more difficult. At one point in the Táin it is only the intercession of Lugh and his sí warriors who intervene to protect and heal Cu Chulainn that prevents his death.

As a prelude to the entire Táin it's important to understand that the events occur because of the curse Macha lays on the men of Ulster, which was previously discussed in the chapter on Macha. This curse lays low the warriors of Ulster when they are in great need, but does not affect Cu Chulainn, either because of his youth or because his father is the God Lugh. This means that when the armies of Connacht attack the only one who can defend Ulster is Cu Chulainn alone. Had Macha's curse not been on the warriors the entire story would have gone much differently.

Cu Chulainn first encounters the Morrigan in the story of the Táin Bó Regamna, after hearing a cow crying out in distress. He searches for the source of the noise and finds a very strange sight: a one-legged horse hitched to a chariot by a pole transfixing its body, with a red-haired, red-cloaked woman in the chariot and a man driving a cow alongside. Cu Chulainn tries to speak to the man, challenging their right to the cow, but the woman answers him, responding that it is none of his business. As the encounter goes on with the woman frustrating the hero with her answers, he eventually leaps onto the woman's shoulders, threatening her with his spear. She tells him she is a satirist – a type of poet – and recites a poem for him. He leaps down and throws a spear at her, only to find that all have vanished and the woman has become a raven perched in a nearby tree.

Recognizing her as the Morrigan he says that if he had known it was her from the beginning the encounter would have gone differently, to which she replies that he will suffer for what he has done. He tells her she has no power over him, but she replies that she does indeed and then tells him that she is guarding his death and will continue to do so. She then incites him to battle, telling him that the cow is hers and that she has taken it out of the sí of Cruachan to breed it to the bull of Cualgne, which will lead to the Táin Bó Cúailgne. She also says that he shall die when the cow's unborn calf is a yearling. He welcomes the battle as something that will increase his glory and fame, denying that he will die in the conflict, and she promises to hinder him in three different forms, as an eel tying his feet, as a wolf biting him, and as an Otherworldly cow leading a host of cows against him. To each threat he replies that he shall overcome her and she will not be healed without his blessing. The two-part ways and the Morrigan returns to the cave of Cruachan.

The Morrigan initially appears in the Táin Bó Cúailgne itself sitting, either in the form of a woman or crow, on a stone pillar near the Brown Bull, the Donn of Cúailgne, who is pastured with his 50 heifers. She speaks to the bull, warning him of the coming cattle raid so that he moves his herd. This is the second time we know of that she has interacted with the bull, the first being alluded to in the previous Táin Bó Regamna.

We first see Badb when she appears to Queen Medb in a dream and incites her to avenge her son, who has been killed. This is reminiscent of the way that the Morrigan appeared to Lugh in the second battle of Maige Tuired and incited Lugh to fight or the way that she appeared to Cu Chulainn in the Táin Bó Regamna and incited him to battle during the future Táin Bó Cúailgne. Inciting warriors to battle is a significant theme for the Morrigan.

When next Cu Chulainn and the Morrigan meet she appears to him in the guise of a beautiful young woman, offering him victory if he will sleep with her. He refuses, saying that he has come for battle not for a woman's body. She later appears while he is fighting as a wolf, eel, and heifer, each time causing him to be injured, but is dealt three blows by the hero which he promises he will never agree to heal. She then appears to him as an old woman with a three-teated dairy cow and offers him milk from the cow; after each drink he blesses her, healing one of her wounds. It may seem odd to us that Cu Chulainn was so easily lured by a simple offer of milk, but we should remember that the early Irish were a heavily dairy based culture. Early Ireland used a wider range of dairy products than most other contemporary cultures and milk especially was enjoyed in a variety of forms (MacCormick, 2008). The offer of fresh milk to a man in the middle of fighting a war was a great temptation indeed, and I believe the story's audience would have understood why he so easily agreed to drink and blessed the woman offering it to him. After the third blessing, when she was completely healed, she reminded him that he had said he would never offer her his blessing and he replied that if he had known it was her, he would not have.

Later in the story Cu Chulainn raises a great shout upon seeing the army gathered to fight him, and Nemain appears, shrieking, along with a multitude of dangerous spirits. Her voice is so terrifying that 100 warriors fall dead at hearing it. Gulermovich Epstein suggests that in the Táin Bó Cúailgne Badb often appears around Cu Chulainn when he is fighting because of several places where the hero references the great noise she makes around him (Gulermovich Epstein, 1998). Nemain then appears again over the opposing army, this time at night, causing confusion and terror, and in some versions bringing prophetic dreams.

The final time we see the Morrigan in this Táin is when she appears to both armies chanting a poem to incite them to battle. She promises both sides victory, apparently genuinely prophesying it to Ulster, but tricking the other army by encouraging the warriors to a fight they were doomed to lose. It is also possible that her poem was not a prophecy at all but a straightforward incitement to battle, a practice among the early Irish called laíded.

Included in the Ulster Cycle, which the Táin Bó Cúailgne belongs to, is the Aided Conculaind, the Death of Cu Chulainn. This story also features the Morrigan in several ways. Before the final battle in which the hero will be killed, the Morrigan appears and breaks his chariot to try to keep him from the fighting, although he seems to perceive it as either a challenge by her or an ill omen. On the morning of the battle his horse, the Grey of Macha, refuses to be harnessed and then cries tears of blood, presaging his death. In some versions of the tale, he sees Badb as a washer at the ford as he goes to battle, and knows she

44

is washing his own bloody battle gear, an omen of his death. During the battle itself the Grey of Macha fights fiercely even after being mortally wounded to defend Cu Chulainn. When the hero is finally wounded to the point of dying, he ties himself to a pillar so that he might remain on his feet and his enemies are so fearful of him that they dare not approach to see if he has died until the story says that: *"And then came the battle Goddess Morrigu and her sisters in the form of scald-crows and sat on his shoulder."* (Jones, 2014). Only when this happens and they are certain he has died do they come forward to claim their trophy. And with this the Morrigan's promise from the Táin Bó Regamna comes to pass as she did indeed guard his death.

The Morrigan in My Life

My first introduction to the Morrigan did not come in ancient epics, nor in modern paganism. No, my first encounter with her came in a children's book in which she was the villain. The book, by Pat O'Shae, is called *The Hounds of the Morrigan* and to this day it is one of my favorites. It is the story of two children, a brother and sister, who set out on an epic journey into the Otherworld with the help of Angus mac Og and his sister Brighid. They have come into possession of a relic which the Morrigan is also seeking because it is the prison for a powerful creature and if she gets hold of it can give her the power to take over the world. In the story the Morrigan appears as a motorcycle-riding old woman with her two sisters and causes havoc and problems for the two children throughout.

It may seem odd that I like the book so much since it paints the Morrigan as the villain, but as a child I was fascinated by the portrayal of her in the book as well as all the other magical and mystical beings in the story. I was never afraid of this fictional Morrigan or her sisters, but rather I found them fascinating in a way that is hard to describe. I didn't want them to win in the story and yet a part of me sided with them and wanted to see them returned to their former glory, only hinted at in the book. Years later I would pick up the threads of the Morrigan's story in real myth and folklore, but that first introduction, through a child's eyes, has always stayed with me.

Chapter Six

Animals and the Morrigan

The Morrigan and her sisters were strongly associated with several different animals. To better understand the meaning of the forms she takes it is helpful to understand the place each animal held in ancient Irish culture. In the story of the Táin Bó Regamna the Morrigan takes the form of a raven and in the story of Da Derga's Hostel Badb appears as a crow. In the Táin Bó Cúailgne the Morrigan changes into a wolf, eel, and heifer when she is fighting against Cu Chulainn. Macha is also associated with crows as well as horses. We will look at each of these animals in turn in the following sections.

Ravens

Called Fiach or Fiach Dubh in Irish, the raven has long been associated with the Morrigan. The raven is one of the forms the Morrigan and Badb are known to take, for example at the end of the Táin Bó Regamna where she transforms into a raven while confronting Cu Chulainn. Ravens were seen as symbols of both war – being birds that were drawn to battlefields and fed on carrion – and of prophecy (Green, 1992). Ravens appear on coins and also on armor, and bones from ravens have been found in sacrificial deposit sites among the continental Celts (Green, 1992).

The raven is a well-known bird of omen. Any time ravens are in the area their activity, calls, and direction of flight might be noted and interpreted, often interpreted as an ill omen. If a raven arrives just as a new task is being begun it is seen as an omen that the work will not end well, and a raven near a home signifies a death (O hOgain, 1995). On the other hand, should a raven with white on its wings fly to the right-hand side of a person and call out it was thought to be a sign of great luck for the person (Anderson, 2008).

Author Glynn Anderson suggests that most Irish lore about the raven is shared by the Norse and reflects Viking influence (Anderson, 2008). In Irish myth ravens are associated with several deities including the Morrigan and Lugh (Anderson, 2008). Ravens are seen as psychopomps who are able to travel between the world of the living and the world of the dead, as well as the Otherworld. They have strong associations as messengers, which may be why they are seen as such powerful birds of omen.

The Hooded Crow

Called Feannóg in Irish, the crow is seen with a similar mix of good and bad omens to ravens. Badb was also called Badb Catha, literally "battle Badb" or "battle crow" and both she and the Morrigan were said to change from human form to crows (Green, 1992). Macha is associated with crows and one meaning of her name is given as Royston crow, an old name for the hooded crow (eDIL, n.d.). When Cu Chulainn died a crow, believed to be one of the Morrigans, appeared and perched on his shoulder to signal his death to his enemies (Green, 1992).

Unlike other types of crows, hooded crows are not solid black, but rather the head, chest, wings, and tail are black and everything else is grey. This gives them a distinct appearance that makes them stand out from their all-black cousins. In the Shetland Islands hooded crows are so common that to see black crows was believed to be an omen of starvation to come (Gulermovich Epstein, 1998). As with ravens, a crow landing on the roof of a house or flying over a home was an omen of death or disaster, but others believe that bad luck comes when crows leave an area (O hOgain, 1995; Anderson, 2008). It was believed that witches, fairies, bansidhe, and Badb appeared as hooded crows in Ireland, a belief that was especially strong in County Clare, and they were thus seen as unlucky (Anderson, 2008). Generally, crows and ravens seem to be treated almost interchangeably in stories.

Wolves

Wolves were significant animals to the Celts long before they came to Ireland, and doubtless played a role for the native Neolithic peoples as well. From archaeological sources we know that the continental Celts hunted wolves for their fur and to use their bones and teeth for jewelry (Green, 1992). In later periods wolves were popular images in artwork as well, appearing alone or paired with deer (Green, 1992). The battle horn, or carnyx, which was blown in battle to create a loud fearsome noise, was sometimes made in the shape of a wolf's head, and warriors' armor was sometimes decorated with images of wolves (Green, 1992). Warriors were also sometimes called wolfsheads, or coinchenn, in Irish (eDIL, n.d.).

Several different sources talk about Celtic tribes that believed they were descended from wolves (Monaghan, 2004). Wolves were also associated with the night-time and the underworld, as well as being an animal connected symbolically with warriors due to its fierceness (Green, 1992; MacCulloch, 1911). Taking all of this information together we can perhaps come to associate wolves with the dead and with the wilderness as well as battle, all things which can easily be related to the Morrigan as well.

Wolves also had a strong association with outlaws and with shapeshifting. The word folc means both wolf and lawless brigand (eDIL, n.d.). In myth there was sometimes an assumption that outlaws could take the form of wolves and in some cases that a person's spirit could fare forth in the form of a wolf (Koch, 2005).

Dogs were the domesticated face of the wolf and it is interesting to note that one of the forms used by the Morrigan when she came at Cu Chulainn, whose name means "the hound of Culan", was that of a wolf. At the time Cu Chulainn was defending Ulster and might be seen to represent right order and honorable behavior, so the Morrigan coming at him in a form associated with outlawry and being outside the bounds of society creates an interesting layer of symbolism to the event.

Eels and Snakes

The Morrigan takes the form of an eel when fighting against Cu Chulainn and it is said that her son Meche has three serpents or snakes in his heart which could have destroyed Ireland. Eels are a native species in Ireland, but snakes are not found there, having been extinct since the last Ice Age. Eels therefore have a definite real-world quality to them, while snakes have a clearly mythic quality to them. Miranda Green in her book *Animals in Celtic Life and Myth* suggests that snakes symbolize death, destruction, evil, healing, fertility, and are connected to water (Green, 1992). Interestingly many Irish stories featuring "snakes" involve water snakes, or snakes living in water, suggesting that Green's association of the two, snakes and water, may have some merit in Irish symbolism.

It is difficult to say why the Morrigan appeared to Cu Chulainn not as a supernatural snake (remember there were no snakes in Ireland so any references to such are clearly discussing a supernatural or Otherworldly element) but as a very natural eel, except that the story may have been emphasizing that she approached him in three forms that represented natural animals. Additionally, Badb is connected to the concepts of serpents and venom, and Nemain's name may mean venomous (Gulermovich Epstein, 1998).

Cows

The cow, bó in Irish, and bull, or tarbh, were significant in many Irish stories because Irish society was based on cattle owning; wealth was measured in cattle and cattle raids were significant events and formed their own branch of literature, called tána. The cow was the backbone of a person's social standing, the basic monetary unit, and was used to settle legal disputes as the means to pay fines (MacCormick, 2008). Within this it is important to realize that certain types of animals had greater values than others, with a milk cow ranking highest (MacCormick, 2008).

Many Irish Goddesses were associated with cows, either appearing in the form of cows, owning magical cows, having cows who gave huge amounts of milk or being reared on milk from a magical cow. When we first see the Morrigan in the form of a cow in the Táin Bó Cúailgne she is described as a hornless red heifer; a heifer is a young cow that has not yet born a calf and would be of less value. Later in the same story she appears as an old woman with a milk cow and uses the produce of the animal to trick Cu Chulainn into healing her after he swore he wouldn't. Cu Chulainn's first meeting with the Morrigan also involved a cow, as he tried to stop her from driving a cow he believed she had stolen and which would eventually set off the events of the famous Táin Bó Cúailgne.

Cattle appear in artwork, symbolizing prosperity and reflecting the herding culture of the Celts (Green, 1992). It is also possible that the design of ringforts was influenced by cattle, as evidence suggests that the structures were used to protect cattle from raiding, or at least that cattle were kept within them (MacCormick, 2008). In a modern context it can be difficult for us to understand exactly how important, how pivotal, cows were in early Irish society. They were money, they were social standing, they were the source of a main food product, they were art motifs and a factor in designing forts. For the Morrigan to appear as a cow and in relation to cows, especially cattle raids, carries a profound significance that it's important for us to at least try to understand.

The Morrigan is associated with cows in several ways. As we have seen she takes the form of a cow and appears with a cow in the Táin Bó Cúailgne. She also steals cows in several stories including the Echtra Nerai and Odras. In the story of Odras the Morrigan steals a bull which a woman named Odras tries to get back. The woman pursues the bull back to the cave of Cruachan but then falls asleep. Finding her this way the Morrigan turns Odras into a river. While her motives in the tale of Odras are hard to understand; usually when she is stealing cows the larger purpose relates to starting cattle raids – effectively starting wars.

Horses

Horses have long been seen as sacred animals in Irish paganism. Evidence shows the presence of horses in Ireland as far back as 3000 BCE and we know that during the Celtic period they played an important role (O hOgain, 2006). Horses were a status symbol, a very practical means of transportation, work animals, and also served in warfare, the Irish fighting mounted and with chariots. Many Irish Gods are associated with horses, including Macha, Aine, Dagda, and Manannan (O hOgain, 2006). Aine, for example, was said to take the form of a red mare and travel around the area near Knockainey. Horses often figure in mythological tales; for example, Cu Chulainn's horses played a role in the Táin Bó Cúailnge, with one of them, the Grey of Macha, weeping prophetic tears of blood before the hero's death. The horses of Donn are said to escort the dead to the Otherworld, by some accounts, and horses were believed to be able to see ghosts and spirits (O hOgain, 2006). Horse skulls and long bones, like human ones, were preserved in ossuaries and there have been archeological finds that included the ritual burial of horses that are believed to have died naturally, showing the importance that the Celts gave to horses (Green, 1992).

Even up until more modern times horse symbolism was important, and we see things like the Lair Bhan (white mare) – a person dressed up in a white sheet holding a carved horse head or skull who led a procession from house to house at Samhain. Holidays like Lughnasa prominently featured horse racing, which might be a race over a flat course or involve the riders swimming the horses across a river. A very old Irish belief was that horses had once been able to speak as humans could and that they were still able to understand people, making it important to always speak kindly to them (O hOgain, 2006).

There are also a wide array of beliefs relating to Otherworldly horses like the Each Uisce and Kelpie; the movie Into the West deals with the story of an Otherworldly horse's relationship with two children in modern Ireland. It was believed that the seventh filly in a row born of the same mare (with no colts in between) was a lucky and blessed animal, called a fiorlair, a true mare (O hOgain, 2006). A true mare was naturally exempt from witchcraft and fairy enchantments, and this protection extended to her rider (Monaghan, 2004). Horses in general were lucky and would be walked over newly ploughed fields, in the belief that a horse trampling freshly planted seed would make the crops grow better (O hOgain, 2006). Many protective charms and superstitions are aimed at protecting horses from the evil eye, fairy mischief and general ill health.

At least one author suggests that eating horse meat was taboo in Ireland except under rare ritual circumstances; although we know that horses were eaten in Gaul and southern England, they did not seem to be considered a food animal in Ireland (Monaghan, 2004; Green, 1992). Reflecting the sacred and important place that horses had in the culture, sites in Gaul that include the remains of sacrificed horses usually also include human sacrificial remains (Green, 1992). We have one anecdotal report of horses being sacrificed and eaten in Ireland, in association with the crowning of a king. A ritual was enacted in Ulster, according to Gerald Cambrensis writing in the 13th century, where the new king had sex with a white mare who was then killed and stewed; the king bathed in the stew and then ate it, as did the gathered people (Puuhvel, 1981). This ritual is assumed to have ties to the horse's symbolism and represented the king joining with the Goddess of sovereignty. This report though is problematic in several ways. It occurred very late into the Christian period, well after the conversion of the country, and the author makes his disdain for the Irish abundantly clear in his book *Topographia Hibernica,* where he says the Irish people are savage and lack any civilization. This makes his story about a barbaric king-making rite with bestiality and sacrificial feasting hard to trust on face value (Wright, 1913).

A Note on Animal Sacrifice and Sacred Animals

Ritual animal sacrifice is a complicated subject in its own right. It is up to the reader to decide whether the practice is allowable within their own spiritual framework. However, it would be wise to respect the practices of others even when they differ from our own. Many people are categorically against the practice, but many others see it as integral to what they do in their attempts to reconstruct or honor the historic faith. I am not going to try to change anyone's opinion on animal sacrifice in general, but I would like to encourage everyone to consider the appropriateness of the choice of animals when it is done.

Although I support traditional religious animal sacrifice in a Celtic context, I am absolutely against sacrificing or eating horses. This is a controversial topic, but my opinion on this is firm. At one time I had held a different view on this, which was born, I must admit, out of a hesitance to judge modern cultures that still eat horses. But the reality is I can judge the practice as wrong – like eating whale, dog, or tiger, which I am also against – without condemning the entire culture that does it.

The ritual recorded by Gerald is a main one used by modern people wanting to do horse sacrifices to defend the idea. However, it should be obvious for several reasons why this ritual does not justify modern horse sacrifice. Firstly, it was rarely done, if we credit Gerald's account, and only on the most significant of events, the crowning of a king and his marriage to the land. We have no modern equivalent to this. Secondly the ritual also involved public bestiality and bathing in the food before it was served; I hope the reasons not to do this are self-evident. Beyond this, as can be seen by the Gaulish examples of interred horse and human sacrifices, the ritual killing of horses seems to have been viewed as an occasion of the utmost gravity, on par with offering a human life. Green theorizes that these events related to the fulfillment of battle pledges, where a warrior going to fight promised to give to the Gods all the spoils of war, including weapons, horses, and human captives in exchange for victory (Green, 1992).

Just as we no longer practice human sacrifice because it goes against our social norms and morality, so too should we leave horse sacrifice in the past. Horses, like dogs, are animals that we have domesticated to work with us and as pets; they are not food. In the past our ancestors may – or may not – have eaten them, but they also had far fewer options than we do; they needed to eat their domestic pets – we don't. It's also important to realize that most domestic animals, especially horses, that are later used for food but are not raised as food animals, are exposed to a variety of chemicals, including painkillers like Phenylbutazone, that are extremely dangerous for humans to consume.

I also feel strongly that it is wrong to sacrifice horses to Macha especially. In Irish myth it is almost always geis (a ritual taboo or prohibition) to eat the animal that represents or is connected to you; Cu Chulainn has a geis against eating dog, Dairmud has a geis not to hunt the boar that is magically bound to him, and Conaire cannot hunt birds, to give some examples. Since horses are Macha's animal it follows that killing or eating them would be offensive to her so they would not be an animal offered to her.

I personally received a geis against eating horse when I became her priestess so I admit to having some bias on the subject but I feel the argument against it is strong. As MacCulloch says in *The Religion of the Ancient Celts*, *"Fatal results following upon the killing or eating of an animal with which the eater was connected by name or descent are found in the Irish sagas."* (MacCulloch, 1911).

Logic would tell us that if it is geis to eat or harm an animal connected to a person in this way then it would hold true that it would also be taboo to sacrifice certain animals to Gods they were strongly associated with. There is also evidence from other Celtic areas that certain animals were not killed or eaten due to their sacred nature or association with specific deities (MacCulloch, 1911). We do not have a single concrete example from myth or folklore of horses being sacrificed to Macha and we do have evidence that killing or eating a symbolic animal was taboo. It is also worth considering that this would hold true for the other Morrigans and their sacred animals as well.

The Morrigan in My Life

Animals can often appear as omens, and the animals of the Morrigan, especially crows and ravens, are seen by many as her messengers, appearing in portentous ways. The important thing with her animals is not only to respect and honor them but also to be aware of them. Not everything is an omen of course, sometimes an eel is just an eel, after all, but if we remain aware of what is going on around us we can catch glimpses of the numinous.

In June of 2014 I was privileged to attend a retreat dedicated to the Morrigan that lasted for three days. The retreat took place at Temenos in Massachusetts, an off-the-grid retreat center. It was an amazing and transformative experience that included rituals to Badb, Macha, and Anu, as well as workshops, music, and fellowship with people who honor the Morrigan from a wide array of pagan traditions and belief systems. We had all come together, some from very far away both in miles and points of view, for that single purpose, and the weekend was a beautiful example of what we can do as a community when we set aside our differences for a common goal.

The entire time I was there I did not see a single crow. I did not hear them calling. I noticed this absence keenly because crows are very common where I live and I am used to seeing and hearing them throughout the day. I had not even realized how used to it I was until I was in a place where they weren't. After the weekend was over, as we were driving away down and off the mountain, we reached a section of road where dirt became pavement, where we transitioned from the sacred space of the retreat to the mundane reality of daily life. As we passed this line three crows flew from right to left across our path and I knew, with absolute certainty, that it was an omen and also a blessing.

Chapter Seven

Finding the Morrigan in the Modern World

The Morrigan in the modern world is at least as complicated as the historical Goddess. Many people today have been called by her and each one will have different views and opinions. In all honesty an entire book could be written just surveying these modern beliefs and still fail to encompass the fullness of her modern interpretations. To some people she is still the historic Goddess, but exists now in a modern context and adapted to the modern world; to others the Morrigan they know bears little resemblance to the ancient Irish Goddess of battle and death.

I do not believe I can tell you how to relate to her or how she might come to you because while she certainly has her own personality that makes her herself and distinct from others, she can also choose how she interacts with each of us. At the end of each previous chapter, I have tried to share bits and pieces of my own feelings and experiences with her and with them to show what a modern relationship can be like. In this chapter I would like to present some further food for thought about relating to the Morrigan in the modern world.

Redefining "Dark" Gods
One of the most pervasive modern views of the Morrigan is that she is a Dark Goddess. Since I have been pagan, I have regularly run across the concept of Dark Gods, usually deities of war, battle, death, or the underworld. The term dark in this case indicates an association between the deity and the aspects of life or the world that people tend to fear; Gods like Kali, Baba Yaga, Odin, Ares, Hecate, and of course the Morrigan are often referred to as being Dark Gods. Some people will advise avoiding such deities altogether while others will say that

approaching them requires extra caution and care. They are said to be less forgiving than other Gods, generally, and harsher. Dark Goddesses often fill the role of Crone in traditions that follow Graves' Maiden-Mother-Crone division of the divine feminine, and Dark Gods are often said to rule over the dark half of the year, further associating them with things that many people perceive as frightening or negative. These ideas can be found in books, websites, and online conversations easily and have become commonplace beliefs in neopaganism. I certainly have fallen into this general line of thinking as a sort of default, even though I am dedicated to deities that are usually described as dark and am a polytheist who follows a different cosmology than mainstream neopaganism.

What I have come to realize is that the entire idea of Dark Gods is, in many ways, an illusion. It is based in a focus on the deities associated with things that we, as modern people, fear because we usually are disconnected from them. Most modern people, especially those with no direct experience of battle and war, look at these concepts as negatives to be avoided, and see the Gods associated with them in a similar light, whereas to our ancestors Gods of battle and war had an important place. Death is feared, especially in our culture where death is often portrayed as an enemy to be fought and most of us are removed from the reality of death since we don't even raise and kill our own food, never mind deal with the hands-on reality of people dying. Even the underworld of the Dark Gods – home of the dead – is seen by some as a place to be avoided because to consider the underworld as a good thing is, on some level, to accept the inevitable death of the self. We fear what these Gods represent and so we fear them.

This view is also rooted in dualism, an approach to deity that would have been foreign to our ancestors (well most of them anyway). It plays into that dreaded either/or mindset that sees everything opposed to something else. To believe in Dark Gods is to, logically, believe in Light Gods, for if the Dark Gods are the ones connected to what we fear then the remaining Gods must be connected to that which we do not fear. When I think about it in these terms, I find it very problematic. The contrast between one group and the other seems to be a reflection of nothing more profound than a modern divine popularity contest, or a reflection of the historic filtering process where the pagan Gods were viewed through a foreign lens and categorized from that perspective.

People say that Dark Gods are harsh when crossed or offended – are the other Gods less so? Doesn't mythology show us that any deity when offended is likely to react badly? People say that Dark Gods are the teachers of hard lessons – but are the other Gods' lessons any easier? Or isn't it just that we can feel more comfortable with a Goddess of healing than a Goddess of battle, even though both deserve equal respect?

It is true that the Gods usually called dark are known for some of their negative interactions with people, yet there are also examples of positive interactions. In the same way the non-dark deities are usually seen as gentle or safe, yet we can often find examples of them acting against our interests or punishing those who offend them. Áine is seen as a Goddess of the sun and fertility by some and yet she is also the consort of Crom Cruach who seeks to steal the harvest each year. The Dagda is a God of wisdom and abundance, yet he possesses a club that can strike eight men dead at one blow. My point here is that the Gods are all complex beings that can never be defined in such broad strokes or absolutes.

There is also the risk with this view of missing important nuances of a deity by focusing exclusively on one narrow aspect of what that God relates to. The Morrigan is not only a Goddess of war. To focus only on her role as a war Goddess is to lose the depth and breadth of her power and personality. Every deity labeled dark is more complex and diverse than any simple label can convey. To approach them otherwise is to reduce the deity to a caricature.

I am devoted to several deities often defined as dark, and yet I do not approach them this way – they are simply the Gods who called to me and who bless my life. Really how can I call dark, with all the implications of that term, powers who have supported my life and responded to my prayers? How could I ever urge people not to honor my Gods, or even to fear them, when they have done so much good for me? Certainly, they deserve to be approached with respect, but that is no more or less true for the Morrigan than it is for Brighid. And when we put so much emphasis on treating one group of Gods with such fear and caution isn't there the danger of becoming lax with the others and treating them with less?

In the future I am not going to divide the Gods this way. I will give all the ones I honor equal respect and treat them with equal caution, and be aware of the tendency to become too comfortable with the "Light" Gods and too fearful of the "Dark" Gods. Because I see now that each individual deity has both dark and light, both positive and negative, within them.

For people just coming to the Morrigan I urge you to think about what the term Dark Goddess means to you. For those who are afraid of her war and battle connections, think about why she brings those feelings out in you. For those who only see her as death and blood, why are you avoiding her other associations? For those who only acknowledge her other qualities and reject her harsh features altogether, ask yourself why you fear her strength. Looking at what she makes us feel and trying to understand why we feel that way can be enormously helpful in creating a stronger connection to her.

"Working with" the Morrigan

There is a common expression in neopaganism, where a person will say that they "work with" certain deities; generally, what they actually mean is either that they worship those deities, or that they call on them for a specific purpose. In my experience among Reconstructionists it is considered disrespectful to say you work with a deity, because however you view the Gods, they are not usually seen as our partners in projects. Patrons, perhaps, or guides, but not partners as another person would be to work with us. It's an interesting bit of semantics between the two approaches to paganism. In neopaganism the phrase is used commonly and doesn't seem to even register with most people, while in Reconstructionist faiths you don't tend to see it used and when it is it can become the focus of the discussion as people debate the accuracy or blasphemy of it. Many neopagans tend to see the entire concept and nature of deity in a way that lends itself to the idea of Gods helping us for no reason except that we ask for the help, while recons tend to see our relationship to deity as based on reciprocity and balance.

I believe that to work with a deity is closer to the client/patron type relationship that is seen in Reconstructionist approaches, where very specific guidelines and goals are needed, and offerings are made, as well as divination to ascertain that the deity involved is willing and agreeable. It goes beyond the patron/client relationship though, in my opinion, because it is more invasive and intense – and I highly recommend setting a very clear time limit. The value is that connecting to, trusting, and allowing a deity to help you on that level is more profound than anything else can be, I believe, and can accomplish things that might otherwise not be achieved. If, of course, you are willing to pay the price of doing it.

In my experience many people initially coming to the Morrigan do so with the idea of working with her in the neopagan context. This is not always the case of course as some people do choose to worship her without the overtones of working with her, but I have found it to be common. In some cases, it's not the person reaching out to her, but rather the Morrigan who makes her presence known to them. Sometimes she comes to a person for a specific purpose and other times she comes and stays, whatever our intentions were going into it. It's always best to remember that once you invite a deity in – in any context – you can never be entirely sure how the relationship will go. It also happens sometimes that a person invites her in but she does not respond to them.

There are many reasons why someone might want to temporarily honor or work with the Morrigan. It is a very old belief that if a God could give something they could also take it away, so the Morrigan who brings terror, battle frenzy/rage, and madness could be prayed to – or worked with – if a person wants relief from those issues. As a Goddess of sovereignty, especially as Macha, she can also be worked with to gain a better sense of self and of self-empowerment. As a Goddess of prophecy, she can help a person gain skill in that area as well. If you choose to work with her, rather than worship her, I suggest setting a time limit and strict guidelines. Agree up front to what you're willing to pay, and know that she always collects.

Modern Altars

One of the first steps in creating a connection to any deity is creating an altar space for them. The altar is a focal point of worship, a place to leave offerings, a place to pray, and a place to go to feel connected. Sometimes an altar will be permanent, other times temporary, but in any case, it serves as an important way for us to create a tangible space to commune with our Gods.

Exactly what is on a modern altar and how the altar is used can vary widely and generally each tradition or faith will have guidelines or expectations for the set-up of an altar. Most altars that I have seen will include sacred images, candles, and a place or bowl for offerings, but some may also include a variety of objects and tools. My own altars tend to get very elaborate as I try to include a variety of things that are important to me, but

I have seen some that are as simple as a candle and incense burner.

Creating an altar for the Morrigan, whether for Anu or one of the other Morrigans, is a very personal thing to do. It should reflect your own understanding of the deity the altar is meant to honor, but basic suggestions would include imagery related to the Goddess or things symbolic of her. For Anu this might include statues of the different animal forms she assumes, while Macha might include horses and crows, and Badb might include crows and ravens. Statues of the Morrigan can also be included and there are several very good ones to be found out there including ones by Dryad Designs and Sacred Source. You can also consider making your own with clay or using pictures or artwork. Beyond that many people include things like swords, spears, or knives, representations of rivers or hills, and sometimes cauldrons. Your altar is your place to connect and worship so it should be set up in a way that speaks to you and works for you.

Prayers, Meditation, and Offerings to the Morrigan

Another way to create or strengthen a relationship with the Morrigan is through regular practices including prayers, meditation, and offerings. I have found it very important for myself to have a regular practice that includes these things and I truly believe that such practices will benefit anyone of any spirituality. They allow us to interact with the Gods we honor in active ways; prayer is speaking to the Gods, meditation is listening to the Gods, and offerings are a way to express tangible gratitude for the blessings in our lives.

I have included a variety of prayers in earlier chapters that you can use, or you can make up your own. I find that people often hesitate to make up their own prayers, but don't be afraid to try. Speaking from your heart and being genuine has more value than the most beautiful prayers recited by rote without any heart. If you are really uncertain you can follow a general guideline of naming who you are praying to, stating something about them, and stating why you are praying to them. For example:

Morrigan, Battle Goddess
Mother of fierce warriors
Inciter of cattle-raids
May I find my fierceness
May my passion be incited
Morrigan, inspire my strength
Let it be so

Meditation can take a variety of forms, from simply calming your mind and being open to messages, to guided meditations, to more involved spiritual journeywork. The most important thing with this is that you do it regularly and allow yourself to be open to listening. My daily meditation practice often consists of walking meditation where I walk and clear my mind and simply listen. It really doesn't have to be more elaborate than that every day, although more rigid types of meditation are also good. The idea is simply to open ourselves up to hear the Gods when they speak, just as prayer is talking to them while they (hopefully!) listen.

Here is an example of a very basic guided meditation to meet the Morrigan:

Sit comfortably where you won't be disturbed. Take several slow, deep breathes. Close your eyes. See yourself walking down a sunlit path through the woods. The trees are heavy around you, the sun filtering in through the leaves. As you walk the trees slowly begin to thin. You realize there is a clearing ahead and you move towards it. The trees open up and you step into an open space, surrounded by a circle of trees. The air is still and silent, as if the world was holding its breath. Into the stillness steps a figure – it is one of the Morrigans. Look at the figure – how does she appear to you? Stepping towards you she tells you her name and gives you a message. Take as long as you need, and when the Morrigan leaves turn and go back down the path. Go back through the tunnel of trees. The trees around you begin to grow denser, thicker as you walk. The light gets darker. Take several deep breathes. Feel yourself fully back in your body. Wiggle your fingers and toes, stretch. Open your eyes when you are ready.

Offerings are a big part of recon faiths but something that can be underemphasized or ignored in some other branches of paganism. I truly believe though that people of all spiritualities can benefit from this practice. An offering is anything given in a sacred way to the Gods or spirits, and this can include physical items like food, incense, or jewelry, or non-physical items like song, poetry and energy. The Morrigan has also been known to take offerings of blood from the person, or offerings of swords and silver. Intent is very important here; offerings should never just be thrown down or hurriedly given but should always be treated in a sacred way. You can say something aloud when you make an offering, such as a prayer, or you can silently focus on what you are doing. Treat the offering as a holy act: take your time, be reverential, be focused, and whether the offering is a small thing or a huge thing give it from your heart.

Generally, if you make offerings, you should have either an offering bowl on your altar to place them in or a special place outdoors to leave them. If its outdoors, make sure the place will not be disturbed by other people and that what you leave won't harm the animals or plants in the area. Tangible offerings can be buried or burned; it was an old Irish and wider Celtic practice that an item being offered would be ritually "killed" in this world by bending or breaking it so that it could never be used again, by a human. This was a way to give it fully to the Gods and is something we can still do today.

Seasonal Celebrations

Another great way to create a connection to the Morrigan, beyond some of the daily or regular practices, is celebrating seasonal rites in her honor. Obviously, you could choose to honor her at any holiday, but she does tend to have associations with certain ones that make those days more appropriate. You can use your imagination in deciding how to incorporate her into your personal celebrations, but these are some ways she relates to different holidays:

- Bealtaine was the day when the Gods arrived in Ireland, and in some versions it was during this time that the three Morrigans used magic against the Fomorians. It is a good time to celebrate the Morrigans as witches, sorceresses, or Druids.
- Midsummer was the date when the Gods fought the Fir Bolg. In the Cath Maige Tuired, during this battle Badb is mentioned, so it might be appropriate to honor Badb now.
- Lughnasa is associated with Macha; fairs were held during this time at her ritual center of Emain Macha. It is a good time to honor Macha as a Goddess of sovereignty and the land.
- Samhain is associated with the second battle of Maige Tuired and it was around this time that the Morrigan joined with the Dagda. It would be appropriate to retell this story and to honor Morrigan as Queen of the Dead or Badb in her role as prophetess.
- Midwinter can possibly be associated with Grian, who may be associated with Macha.

Reconstructing Celtic Seership with Badb

I consider seership a significant part of my practice because I see the taking of omens as essential in ritual. I also keep in mind the Irish triad which says: "Three signs of wisdom: patience, closeness, the gift of prophecy." (Meyers, 1906). In my book *Where the Hawthorn Grows* I discuss my approach to Irish seership practices, but I don't talk about what I actual do, so here I thought I'd talk about my reconstruction and practice of three methods of Irish seership and how they relate to my honoring of the Morrigan.

There were three specific seership practices written about in Ireland and these were imbas forosna – "manifesting knowledge", tenm laida – "illumination of song", and dichetal do chennaib – "extemporaneous poetry" (Matthews, J., 1999). Each of these methods is somewhat obscure and requires both research and inspiration to make usable in a modern context. I firmly believe though that it is possible to reconstruct these methods in effective ways.

Imbas forosnai involves preparing and eating meat (pig, cat, or dog historically or pig today), making an offering to the Gods with specific chants and then lying down with the hands covering the eyes and sleeping or meditating for up to three days undisturbed to receive knowledge or an answer. Another well-known version of this may be the tarbh feis, which involves the sacrifice of a bull, eating its flesh and then wrapping up in its hide for the same purpose. The practice of retreating into a dark room, wrapped in a cloak to receive inspiration – possibly a later version of imbas forosnai, I think – was seen in the Scottish Highlands until a few hundred years ago (Bell, 1703).

For the purposes of modern practice, I use two versions of this method. The first is closer to the later Scottish version; I lie down in a darkened room, beneath a cloak, cover my eyes and enter a meditative trance state while focusing on the question I am trying to answer. The second is closer to the older descriptions of imbas forosnai and takes more time and preparation, beginning with cooking a pork roast. In the original ritual the meat was eaten raw, but for modern purposes and safety reasons I cook mine. Some of the pork is ritually offered to Badb8, who I call on for prophecy, and some is eaten by me. I have special prayers I say to her. After eating the meat, I go somewhere quiet, and pray:

> Badb, who sees what has not yet come to pass
> Who spoke the great prophecy when the battle
> Between the Tuatha De and the Fomorians ended
> Who spoke of both great peace and an end to all
> Help me now to see what I need to see
> To find the answer to the question I have
> Open the way for me to receive my answer

I lay down in a comfortable position and cover my eyes with my hands. To enter into a trance state, I repeatedly chant to myself:

> Badb Goddess of prophecy
> May I see the past and the future
> May I know the Truth of what is
> May I find what I seek, and speak it
> Badb, open the way for me
> To see, to know, to speak
> To prophecy of what was and
> What is, and what will be
> Badb, Goddess of prophecy
> May it be so

After repeating this over and over I eventually fall into a trance where I receive the answer. Sometimes it may come as words or a direct message, other times as images.

Tenm laida seems to be, based on its appearance in myths, a type of light trance that a person could enter to answer specific questions, sometimes associated with touching the object directly and other times with putting the tips of the fingers or thumb in the mouth, such as in the stories of Finn mac Cool. In some stories it appears as a method to read the past or identify a body, although this also appears to be a type of seership practiced by both Scathach and Fidelm in mythology when answering questions about the future (Matthews, J., 1999). This method reminds me strongly of psychometry and my own version is very similar to that modern practice. Both imbas forosnai and tenm laida were outlawed by the Christian Church for calling on "idols", so when I use tenm laida I begin with a short chant to the Gods and spirits based on my version of an augury charm:

Gods over me, Gods under me,
Gods before me, Gods behind me,
Knowledge of truth, not knowledge of falsehood,
That I shall truly see all I search for.
Kindly spirits and Gods of life,
May you give me eyes to see all I seek,
May I see and speak truly

Then I either touch the object or put my hands to my mouth and open myself to what comes. This method, naturally, takes a great deal of practice, but it's actually a fun one to use that can be done just for practice, as opposed to the other two methods, which require either more ritual or a higher degree of trance and aren't used as lightly. The real trick with tenm laida is learning to open yourself to the impressions and information that comes when you ask and get accurate results; the tendency can be to fall into imagination or to be so self-critical that you can't relax enough to receive anything.

The third method is dichetal do chenaib, which seems to resemble tenm laida but involve a deeper trance and the spontaneous speaking of poetry to answer the question. Perhaps the Prophecy of the Morrigan could be viewed as this type of method. Dichetal do chenaib was not outlawed as it didn't directly call on pagan deities or spirits and was seen as a part of the poet's art. Dichetal do chenaib requires spontaneous recitation of poetry, which by itself is both a challenge and an art form. When I use this method, I go into a trance and wait to see what answer comes to the question, and then do my best to channel that answer into a coherent poetic response. I like to use a form where the last word in one "line" is the first word in the next, creating an internal rhythm to the response. I admit though that I find this method the hardest of the three to actually use and so tend to use it the least.

The Morrigan in My Life

My first direct experience with the Morrigan occurred in the context of working with her, when I went to her/them and asked for help in overcoming certain fears and past traumas that I felt were holding me back. I knew that it was an old belief that those deities who could bring or cause a thing could also cure that thing, which is why I chose the three Morrigans to go to in order to deal with those negative feelings that they were so strongly associated with. I did it out of sheer naivety and with no idea of the profound repercussions that would unfold, but in the long run I am glad that I did it. I say during that time I worked with her, but perhaps it's more accurate to say that they worked with me – like clay being worked by a sculptor.

Unlike the more well-known patron dynamic this involved a great deal of direct influence, that might be called hands-on, and is not similar to any other type of relation to deity I have ever had, from casual worship to out-right dedication. The cost of the experience was high, but I believe the result was far more than I ever could have accomplished on my own, so I do think that this type of work has value, if it's entered into with the right mindset and understanding of the consequences. Of course, knowing better now I advise caution before jumping into that sort of thing. In my case I spent six months with my entire life in chaos and was made to confront some of my greatest fears, in reality, in a way that re-shaped who I was as a person on more than one level, and effected changes that are still lasting more than 15 years later. I am a different person now than I was then, because of that "work".

Conclusion

The Morrigan, in many guises, is active in the world today. She is seeking people – not only warriors, but many different kinds of people – to honor her, to speak her name again, to bring her worship into the modern world. She is a powerful presence just as she always has been.

Looking at the historic evidence we can see that the Morrigan is a Goddess who appears in many stories as an instigator of war and inciter of battle. She causes conflict and urges warriors on, as well as predicting the outcomes of battles. In some cases, she also interferes directly in those outcomes, appearing and offering victory to one side if they will pay her price, or in other cases working to aid the side she favors to ensure their victory. She is a Goddess of strategy who plans far in advance and maneuvers things to create situations and results which she wants. She is associated with many animals, but perhaps none more strongly than cattle and crows, which feature prominently in many of her stories. She is ultimately a Goddess of war, but war as the ancient Irish understood it, *"...in her various forms she embodies ... crech: glory and horror, the carnage, the noble beauty, the plundering, the sense of fatal destiny, the noise, the fury."* (Gulermovich Epstein, 1998).

Alongside the Morrigan we have her sisters Macha and Badb who are complexes Goddesses in their own right and also bear the title of Morrigan. Where the Morrigan is associated most strongly with cattle, Macha is connected equally strongly to horses and Badb to crows; all three together share a connection to crows and ravens. Macha is a Goddess of sovereignty, battle, and the land while Badb is a Goddess or battle, prophecy, and terror. All three of the Morrigans are war and death deities and when they appear together it is most often in contexts relating to those subjects.

Besides the three Morrigans there are several other Goddesses who often share the title of Morrigan or are mentioned in relation to it. Each of these may or may not actually be one of the Morrigans, but understanding who they are and why they are connected to that title is important to better understanding who and what the Morrigan is. It is no simple thing to look at the complex web of relations between the different Irish Goddesses in mythology and try to conceptualize how each relates to the other and, more importantly, how certain names which are also titles might apply in different ways. In the same way we can look at the different animal forms that the Morrigans take and the symbolic value of those animals in order to gain a better understanding of the depth of these complex Goddesses.

Connecting to the Morrigan is a lifelong process. Learning about her history and her place in mythology is one step. Reading about another person's experiences with her is another step, as is creating an altar or shrine to her and praying to her regularly. But the next step is to experience her for yourself. If you hear her call, take what you have learned here and let yourself create that connection. Be bold. Be brave. Be her raven.

Bibliography

Anderson, G., (2008) *Birds of Ireland: Facts, Folklore & History*

Banshenchus (n.d.) *Book of Leinster*. Retrieved from http://www. maryjones.us/ctexts/banshenchus.html

Bell, M., (1703) *A Description of the Western Isles of Scotland*

Berresford Ellis, P., (1987) *A Dictionary of Irish Mythology*

Bonevisuto, N., (2014) *By Blood, Bone, and Blade: A Tribute to the Morrigan*

Chadwick N., (1935) *Imbas Forosnai*. Retrieved from http:// searchingforimbas.blogspot.com/p/imbas-forosnai-by-norakchadwick.html

Clark, R., (1990) *The Great Queens: Irish Goddesses from the Morrigan to Cathleen Ni Houlihan*

Coe, E., (1995) *Macha and Conall Cernach: A Study of Two Iconographic Patterns in Medieval Irish Narrative and Celtic Art*

Cross, T., and Slover. H., (1936) *Ancient Irish Tales* Electronic Dictionary of the Irish Language, eDIL, (n.d.) Retrieved from http://edil.qub.ac.uk/dictionary/search.php

Fraser, J., (1915) *The First Battle of Moytura*

Gray, E. (1983) *Cath Maige Tuired*

Green, M., (1992) *Dictionary of Celtic Myth and Legend*

Green, M., (1992) *Animals in Celtic Life and Myth*

Gregory, A., (1904) *Gods and Fighting Men*

Gulermovich Epstein, A., (1998) *War Goddess: The Morrigan and her Germano-Celtic Counterparts*. Electronic version, #148, September, 1998. Retrieved from http://web.archive.org/ web/20010616084231/members.loop.com/~musofire/diss/

Gwynn (1924) *The Metrical Dindshenchas*

Harper, D., (2014) *Danube*. Retrieved from http://www. etymonline.com/index.php?term=Danube&allowed_in_ frame=0

Heijda, K., (2007) *War Goddesses, Furies, and Scald Crows.* University of Utrecht

Hennessey, WM. (1870) *The Ancient Irish Goddess of War.* Retrieved from http://www.sacred-texts.com/neu/celt/aigw/index.htm

Jones, M., (2009) *Anu.* Retrieved from http://www.maryjones.us/jce/anu.html

Jones, M., (2008) *Macha.* Retrieved from http://www.maryjones.us/jce/macha.html

Jones, M., (2014) *Tain Bo Regamna.* Retrieved from http://www.maryjones.us/ctexts/regamna.html

Jones, M., (2014) *Aided Conculaind.* Retrieved from http://www.maryjones.us/ctexts/cuchulain3.html

Keating, G., (1908) *The History of Ireland.* Retrieved from http://www.ucc.ie/celt/online/T100054/

Koch, J., (2005) *Celtic Culture, a Historical Encyclopedia*

Kondratiev, A., (1998) *Danu and Bile – Primordial Parents?* Retrieved from http://www.imbas.org/articles/danu_bile.html

Lambert, K., (2014) *The Irish War Goddesses.* Retrieved from http://dunsgathan.net/caithream/warGoddesses.html

Macalister, R. (1941) *Lebor Gabala Erenn*, volume IV

MacCulloch, J. (1911) *The Religion of the Ancient Celts.*

MacCulloch, J. (1918) *Celtic Mythology*

MacKillop, J., (1998) *Dictionary of Celtic Mythology*

Matthews, J., (1999) *Celtic Seers Sourcebook*

McCormick, F., (2008) *The Decline of the Cow: Agricultural and Settlement Change in Early Medieval Ireland*

McNeill, M., (1962) *Festival of Lughnasa*

Meyers, K., (1906) *The Triads of Ireland.* http://www.ucc.ie/celt/online/T103006.html

Monaghan, P., (2004) *An Encyclopedia of Irish Mythology and Folklore*

O Donaill (1977) *Focloir Gaeilge-Bearla*

O hOgain, D., (2006) *The Lore of Ireland*

O hOgain, D., (1995) *Irish Superstitions*

O'Rahilly, C., (2001) *Tain Bo Cualnge Recension 1.* Retrieved from http://www.ucc.ie/celt/published/T301012/index.html

Puuvel, J., (1981) "Aspects of Equine Functionality"

Sjoestedt, M. (2000) *Celtic Gods and Heroes*

Smyth, D. (1988) *A Guide to Irish Mythology*

Squire, C. (2000) *The Mythology of the British Islands: An Introduction to Celtic Myth, Legend, Poetry and Romance*

Stokes, W., (1891) *Second Battle of Moytura*

Woodfield, S., (2011) *Celtic Lore & Spellcraft of the Dark Goddess: Invoking the Morrigan*

Wright, T., (1913) *The Historical Works of Giraldus Cambrensis*

Endnotes

1   Anu and Anand or Anann are the same name just as Danu and Danand or Danann are the same name. The difference between the –u ending and –nn ending is created by the case that the name is in when written in Irish Gaelic. Also, at some point the Old Irish ending –nd shifted to a double –nn creating the change from Anand to Anann. So, while the names look different and can seem confusing to English speakers the two sets represent different versions of two single names. In English these are most commonly given as Anu and Danu, respectively.

2   A prohibition of silence regarding an Otherworldly spouse is not an uncommon theme in fairylore. Generally, such spouses will have some unusual rule that the human spouse must follow, and if broken the fairy returns immediately back from whence they came.

3   Halidom means a sacred place or thing.

4   Beannighe – the washer-at-the-ford type fairy.

5   Versicles are short chants or songs.

6   Danu is from the Celtic root Danu(w)yo from the proto-Indo-European Danu meaning river (Harper, 2014).

7   I recommend Michelle Skye's series of books, *Goddess Alive, Goddess Afoot,* and *Goddess Aloud* for some good guided meditations, several of which deal with the Morrigans, if you are interested.

8   After being offered and left on the altar during the ritual it is later given to the crows outside.

PAGAN PORTALS

RAVEN GODDESS

Going Deeper with the Morrigan

MORGAN DAIMLER

Pagan Portals

Raven Goddess

Going Deeper with the Morrigan

Morgan Daimler

What People Are Saying About

Raven Goddess

There are no shortages of misconceptions about The Morrigan. Perhaps even more so now that she is a popular figure in modern Paganism. Daimler untangles many of our modern assumptions about this power goddess and takes readers on a deeper exploration of her lore. *Raven Goddess* is an excellent resource for all those seeking the Great Queen.

Stephanie Woodfield, author of *Celtic Lore and Spellcraft of the Dark Goddess* and *Dark Goddess Craft*

Raven Goddess: Going Deeper with the Morrigan is an excellent follow-up to Daimler's 2014 Pagan Portals book *The Morrigan: Meeting the Great Queens*. It provides new and more complete translations of key source material, and it clears up some of the misinformation about the Morrigan from both inaccurate scholarship and from modern pop culture. It provides helpful guidelines for deepening your connections to the Morrigan, who is one of the most active Goddesses in our world today. Highly recommended for beginners, but the translations alone are worth the price of the book for anyone.

John Beckett, author of *The Path of Paganism* and *Paganism in Depth*

CONTENTS

This book is dedicated to all of the people out there who look to the trí Morrignae for wisdom, guidance, or inspiration. May you find what you are looking for and always have strength for every fight.

With special thanks to Lora for all the hard work and effort at educating the community.

Tá tú maoin, a chara

Foreword

Daimler has done it again.

Look, folks, ye know I always recommend going to native sources, first and foremost, for all sorts of good and righteous reasons. It's an important thing you could – or even should – be doing, in order to be respectful and walk in Right Relationship with the culture you wish to gain from, to learn from.

Morgan's work is a notable exception. There simply isn't another non-Irish Pagan writer who stands in better relationship with the Gods and Ungods of Ireland, as far as I can see. Their existing body of work on Pagan topics is one I recommend, and indeed refer to and learn from myself, time and time again.

And now this.

Another book dedicated to the Goddess I work for. A companion and expansion to their excellent previous book *The Morrigan: Meeting the Great Queens*. This one truly opens up the information that is available on the Irish Goddess of Battle and Prophecy, shows how much more there is to Her, and Her sisters; in the lore and in the author's personal experience.

In this work you will find guidance to facilitate your own study of the source material. You'll find real information and clarity on what exactly is, and isn't, truly known about the Morrigan. You'll find out what she looks like, what colours and tools are associated with Her, and how to correctly spell Her name. You're going to learn about Her relationship with the Dagda, and the other Beings that move around Her stories. Daimler also breaks down Her involvement in one of the major sagas – the Battle of Moytura (Cath Maige Tuired), and goes on to examine the place of this Goddess in the modern world, and how to connect to Her here and now.

All in all, I know this book will become an invaluable reference work that I keep right at my desk at the Irish Pagan School HQ, alongside so many of Morgan's other books. It is a fantastic addition to the few quality books and resources on this Goddess that I can wholeheartedly recommend.

Lora O'Brien, author of *A Practical Guide to Irish Spirituality: Sli An Dhraoi,* and *A Practical Guide to Pagan Priesthood.*

Preface

This book is intended as a follow up to the previous *Pagan Portals – the Morrigan* but may also be read as a stand-alone work.

I have been an Irish-focused pagan since 1991 and was dedicated to the Morrigan for over a decade. Although in the last three years my focus has shifted more fully to the Daoine Maithe she is still an important deity to me. After writing my previous book *Pagan Portals – the Morrigan* in 2014 I have long debated writing a follow up with a tighter focus on the Morrigan herself and which would tackle some common misconceptions about her in ways that, hopefully, will allow people to develop a deeper, stronger relationship with her.

In writing this I have drawn on many different sources and have carefully referenced and cited all of them. My own degree is in psychology so I prefer to use the APA method of citations. This means that within the text after quotes or paraphrased material the reader will see a set of parentheses containing the author's last name and date the source was published; this can then be cross references with the bibliography at the end of the book. I find this method to be a good one and I prefer it over footnotes or other methods of citation which is why it's the one I use. I have also included end notes in some places where a point needs to be expanded on or further discussed but where it would be awkward to do that within the text itself.

As I have said before in my previous book *Pagan Portals – the Morrigan* I do not think that the religious framework we use to connect to the Gods matters as much as the effort itself to honour the old Gods I think we can all do this respectfully and with an appreciation for history without the need for any particular religion. Whether we are Reconstructionists, Wiccans, or Celtic pagans all that really matters is that we are approaching our faith with sincerity and a genuine intention. To that end this book is written without any specific spiritual faith in mind, beyond polytheism, and it is up to the reader to decide how best to incorporate the material. My own personal path is rooted in witchcraft and reconstruction so that is bound to colour some of my opinions in the text, however, so the reader may want to keep that in mind.

Pagan Portals – Raven Goddess was written as a resource for seekers of the Morrigan specifically and offers both solid academic material and practical advice on connecting with her in a format that is accessible and designed to be easy to read, although it does contain a lot of academic references to older mythology. It is meant to be a follow up to the previous *Pagan Portals – the Morrigan* and take a deeper look into details of this fascinating deity.

For some people this book may be one step in a lifelong journey, an attempt to better understand or connect to a Goddess who is both easily accessible and maddeningly hard to comprehend. For others this book may simply provide another viewpoint of the Morrigan, her history, and modern beliefs and practices associated with her. In either case I hope that the reader feels that some value is gained from the time spent with this short text, getting to know the Morrigan in a deeper sense.

Introduction

The Morrigan is not only a complex deity but one who inspires great passion in people today and there are many different viewpoints of Her to be found. In my previous book I tried to maintain as much objectivity as possible and simply off er the best information I could at the time of who and what she was, as well as relaying information about deities closely connected to her; in this work I am trying to maintain that same level of quality but am taking a more subjective approach. This is the Morrigan through both study and my own experiences over the last 15 years or more.

The Morrigan is one of the most popular Irish goddesses and there is a lot of information to be found about her from a variety of sources. Despite this it can be very difficult to find solid resources about her as the material available is almost overwhelming in quantity now but ranges so widely in quality that trying to sort out the valuable from the dross becomes an enormous task. Misinformation abounds and is quickly repeated and then taken as fact. A great deal of in-depth study is required to sort out opinions from facts, modern invention from older myth, and misunderstanding or mistranslation from quality sources. It's all a bit dizzying especially for those just starting out.

The Morrigan shows up as only a small section in some books taking on the subject of the Irish or Celtic Gods more generally; in older pagan works it wasn't uncommon to find her barely a footnote in the text with a warning against any engagement. This almost phobic reaction to the Morrigan has shifted particularly in the 21st century and with that shift we see a proliferation of sources especially online. In the last decade or so there have been several good books that have come out on the market many of them aimed at offering readers a solid introduction to the Great Queen. My own *Pagan Portals – the Morrigan* had such an aim, but there is also Stephanie Woodfield's *Celtic Lore & Spellcraft of the Dark Goddess: Invoking the Morrigan*, Morpheus Ravenna's *Book of the Great Queen*, and Courtney Weber's *The Morrigan: Celtic Goddess of Magick and Might*. Each of these has its own unique approach and particular books will work better for people from different backgrounds.

As we connect to a deity and work with them and devote ourselves to them, we will find ourselves on a rollercoaster ride of experience and information. I have always found the best approach is to ground the two together, to look for sources to support my experiences and to embrace my experiences as an outgrowth of my deepening understanding. With that in mind as we move forward with this text, I want to include a blend of academic material and my own thoughts on the Morrigan. Whether you agree with everything I have to say or not I hope this will all serve as food for thought for you to develop your own relationship with her. Never stop questioning.

She speaks as often in poetry as prose, so let me end this introduction with this poem which I wrote years ago after the dream it describes:

I dreamed last night –
dream or vision or something more –
of ravens and bloody rivers,
hounds and horses coursing,
pounding hooves and howling voices,
Herself crying "Woe to those who flee!
Blood and battle is upon them!
The fight is upon you!
Stand your ground! Stand and fight!
Hard slaughter and a great victory!"
Her voice and the roaring of a river,

water and blood mixing,
and hounds and horses,
Introduction
and riders armed and armored,
A feeling of panic and joy
of despair and ecstasy joined
twisting together in my gut
until I wanted to rush forward
into any danger, throw myself,
heedless, into madness and battle,
blades clashing, water rushing,
screams of war and death together,
ravens' wings tearing the air
My breath coming in gasps and gulps,
too winded to add my voice to the din,
but pushing forward, forward, further,
each step a success as earth
become mud as it mixed with blood.
And then, abruptly, the dream was gone
I woke to stillness.
No blood. No battle.
No death. No river.
But a yard full of black birds
their voices strident and discordant
singing to me of dreams and shadows
I moved through the day
expecting wings and warriors
the vision like a memory of feathers
which irritates and soothes simultaneously
and, again and again, ceaseless as the tide,
Or a fast flowing stream,
Her voice calling "Awake! Arise!"...

Chapter 1

Towards a Deeper Understanding

As we take our first step into a greater understanding of the Morrigan let us begin by seeking a better understanding of who she is and of things associated with her that are not discussed as often. In this chapter we will look at physical descriptions of the Morrigan in source material, colours connected to her, and her association with a more obscure item. All of this is presented for the reader to consider and weigh against their own experiences and opinions.

Description

A common question that I hear people asking is what does the Morrigan look like, so let's begin with that. There is, of course, a great deal of artwork to be found based in each artist's imagination but let's move past these modern conceptions to find a base to build outwards from. Looking at what we know from mythology and folklore we find a complicated answer. This is because generally when she appears in mythology she is not described in much detail. Instead, we get passages like this one from the Cath Maig Tuired:

> *The Unish of Connacht calls by the south. The woman was at the Unish of Corand washing her genitals, one of her two feet by Allod Echae, that is Echumech, by water at the south, her other by Loscondoib, by water at the north. Nine plaits of hair undone upon her head.*

Similarly, when she appears in most versions of the Táin Bó Cúailnge[1] (TBC) it simply says *"Then came the Morrigan daughter of Ernmas from out of the Sídhe"* without adding any physical details. There are a few appearances which are described however.

In the Táin Bó Regamna (TBR) we are given this:

> *A red-haired woman with red eyebrows was in the chariot with a red cloak around her shoulders; the cloak hung down at the back of the chariot and dragged on the ground behind her.*

This description of a red-haired woman[2] may be the most detailed description we ever get of the Morrigan's physical appearance and it is the only one where we are never told that she is in disguise or in an assumed form. In my own opinion this is most likely to be her true appearance, but other people may have different conclusions. In the Cath Magh Rath she is described as:

> *Bloody over his head, fighting, crying out*
> *A naked hag, swiftly leaping*
> *Over the edges of their armor and shields*
> *She is the grey-haired Morrigu*

This description is somewhat similar to another of the Morrigan's appearances in the TBC: "*then came the Morrigan daughter of Ernmas from out of the Sí shaped as an old woman*". However, this passage makes it clear this is not her natural appearance but a "*richt*", a guise, form, or assumed shape. The idea of the Morrigan taking on other shapes or disguises is a common one, and in fact in the Metrical Dindshenchas she is called "*samla día sóach*" (a phantom, the shape-shifting Goddess) making it clear that her form is fluid and changeable.

It is debatable whether or not the brief description of the Morrigan in disguise as "*Buan's daughter*" in the TBC reflects her true appearance or is, as with her form as an old woman, merely a disguise. In this passage, which does not occur in all versions of the TBC she is described as *"young woman with a garment of every coloring around her and a form fiercely beautiful on her"*. Personally, I'm a bit suspicious because of the phrase *"delb ... furri"* that is "a shape ... on her". It is possible that it's just an expression, or perhaps it could be an allusion to the fact that the Morrigan has assumed this alluring disguise as part of her attempt to trick Cu Chulainn, who has of course seen her red-haired form in the TBR previously.

She also has several animal forms which are described in the TBC as *"a smooth, black eel"*, *"a rough, grey-red [wolf] bitch"*, *"a white, red-eared heifer"* and in the TBR we see these forms echoed in her threats to Cu Chulainn: *"an eel"*, *"a blue-grey[3] wolf-bitch"*, and *"a white, red-eared heifer"* as well as *"a black bird"*. In the Lebor na Huidre she is also described as taking the form of a bird *"the Morrigan, she in the likeness of a bird"*. It is interesting to note that most of these animal depictions come with a specific color.

The Morrigan is clearly capable of assuming many forms to serve her purposes, and we have descriptions of many of them. I have only touched on some here to illustrate what we generally know about her appearance. It may be that her true form is of a red-haired woman dressed in red, as we see in the TBR, but certainly she is not limited to that. She comes to us in many shapes and forms, through many guises and many means. Ultimately, she is what she chooses to seem to be to each viewer, whether that is black bird or white cow, naked hag or fiercely beautiful young woman. She is Herself.

Colors and the Morrigan

It's an interesting thing that many of us who follow, work with, honor, or are otherwise connected to the Morrigan tend to associate her with the colors, red, white, and black. At first one may wonder why, as there isn't any straightforward text or piece of evidence that says 'the Morrigan's colors are such and such'. However, if we look at the total of the evidence, that is all the textual references that mention her and also mention color, we can see some patterns that may explain it.

Directly relating to the Morrigan we admittedly have only a few pieces of color related evidence, but we do have some.

From the Táin Bó Regamna:

> "*A red-haired woman with red eyebrows was in the chariot with a red cloak around her shoulders*"
> "*...he saw that she was a black bird on a branch near him.*"
> "*I will be a blue-grey wolf-bitch then against you,*" she said.
> "*I will be a red-eared white heifer then,*" said she...

From the Táin Bó Cúailnge:

> "*...a smooth, black eel*"
> "*...a rough, grey-red bitch*"
> "*...a white, red-eared heifer*"

From the Cath Mag Rath:

> "*She is the grey-haired Morrigu*"

Additionally, we see Badb referred to repeatedly as 'red-mouthed' or 'the Red Badb', for example here in the Cath Maige Tuired Cunga: "*The Red Badb will thank them for the batt le-combats I look on.*". In the Tochmarc Ferbe Badb is described as a 'white woman' or 'shining woman' and in the Destruction of De Choca's Hostel she is also said to be red-mouthed and pale. Black would be associated with her through ravens and crows.

Macha, has less blatant references to color so more guesswork is required. As Macha Mongruadh [Macha of the red-mane] she would seem to be associated with the color red, something we may also with less surety say due to her being called 'the sun of womanhood' in the Rennes Dindshenchas. Her association with skull could perhaps give us the color white for her, although that in itself is an assumption based on her explicit connection to severed heads and the wider Celtic cultural use of skulls. Black is easier as she is clearly connected to crows and ravens, and grey is also a color connected to her through the hooded crow and through the most famous horse known to be hers [before he was known to be Cu Chulainn's] the Liath Macha, literally 'Macha's Grey'.

All three of the Morrigans [Morrigan, Badb, and Macha] are said to take the form of hooded crows, birds which are black and light grey, and of ravens or crows more generally. In several stories including the Táin Bó Cúailnge the Morrigan is said to appear *"in the form of a bird"* and one may perhaps assume the bird here was meant to be understood as a hooded crow or raven. In the Sanas Cormaic they are called the *"three Morrigans"* and later *"raven women"*. In one version of the Aided Conculaind we are told *"And then came the battle goddess Morrigu and her sisters in the form of scald-crows and sat on his shoulder"*. The names Badb and Macha are also words in Irish that mean crows or hooded crows, reinforcing the connection between the Morrigan(s) and the color black as well as grey.

For the curious a quick summary of the color meanings in old Irish, beyond the actual colors:

- Black had connotations of dark, dire, melancholy, and was used to express intensity, something like the word 'very' in English.
- White represented purity, brightness, holiness, truth but also bloodlessness and was sometimes used to describe

corpses. It was also a color in combination with red that was often used to describe Otherworldly animals.

- Red[4] was used to describe things that were bloody, passionate, fiery, fierce, proud, guilty (think red cheeks) also used as an intensive.
- Grey usually represents age, in the plural the word for the color means 'veterans'.

So, we can see that when color is mentioned in association with the Morrigan it is usually red or black, and slightly less often white or grey, and rarely blueish-green. I might suggest that people who associate red, black, and white with her are either consciously or subconsciously picking up on these patterns from her stories, particularly of the colors of her animal forms when contesting with Cu Chulainn in the Táin Bó Cúailnge which are black (eel), red (wolf), and white (cow), although the red/black/white pattern is not limited to that. Badb and Macha share these color associations in different ways, indicating that it is not the Morrigan as a singular being for which these colors are important but rather that all three Morrigans relate to them.

Fulacht na Morrigna

One of the mysterious things that the Morrigan is associated with is called the fulacht na Morrigna, literally the Morrigan's cooking hearth. A fulacht is a type of outdoor cooking hearth or pit; the smaller ones were named for the Fíanna but the larger ones for the Morrigan (RIA, 1870). These fulachta were associated both with large outdoor stone cooking hearths and with cooking spits, so interchangeably in the texts and academic material that one might assume the two were parts of a single whole. Specific types of wood were associated with the fulacht, particularly in the law texts with the fulacht fían, and these included holly and rowan (Ó Néill, 2003). One might note that one of Cu Chulainn's geasa was not to eat at a fulacht, and this is exactly what he ended up doing after encountering the three crones cooking on rowan spits at a fulacht who offered him hospitality – which he also had a geis not to refuse (Ó Néill, 2003).

We are given descriptions of the Morrigan's fulachts in the Yellow Book of Lecan:

The cooking hearth of the Morrigan is thus that is a portion of raw meat and enjoined of cooked meat and a small portion buttered and nothing melting from the raw flesh and nothing of it burnt by the cooking and at the same time together the trio on the spit.

And also, in a very early Scott ish text (utilizing Old Irish) which describes both the Morrigan's fulacht and the Dagda's anvil excerpted here:

Cooking pit of the Morrigan is thus that is a wood wheel and wood axle between fire and water and an iron body and two people raise the wheel. Smoothly and quickly it went around. Thirty spits projected from it and thirty bars and thirty stakes. A sail on it, and a wonder its form when its bars and wheels were in motion. The Fulacht of the Morrigan very sharp edge of a smith. (Celt. Rev. viii 74; translation mine)

The cooking pit appears in a story recounted in the Agallamh Beg:

It was they who made for themselves a shelter there that night, and made a cooking place by them, and Cailte and Findchadh went to wash their hands in the stream.

"There is a cooking pit" said Findchadh, "and it has been long since its making."

"It is true, said Cailte, "and this is a cooking hearth of the Morrigan, and is not built without water." (RIA, 1870; translation mine)

Archaeological evidence supports the existence of these ancient fulachts which are found across Ireland, and some of the larger ones are considered fulachta na Morrigna with one known of at Tara and one in Tipperary (Martin, 1895). Ó Néill suggests that the fulacht was actually only the wooden portion of the cooking spit and that rather than a fi re pit as we would imagine one it actually involved the use of heated stones for cooking (Ó Néill, 2003). He uses a description of the Fían utilizing a fulacht in Keating's Foras Feasa ar Eirinn as well as archaeology to support this; in Keating's account the fulacht was used not only for cooking but also to simultaneously heat water for washing after a morning of hunting so that the warriors would be clean before eating (Ó Néill, 2003). This theory is intriguing and fits the evidence well, explaining why the Morrigan's fulacht was said to need both fi re and water; the spits would be used for cooking meat over a fi re while heated stones were taken and used to make the water suitable for bathing, as well potentially for boiling food. Since the wood and water would obviously be long gone the only hard evidence left behind would be exactly what we do find at the sites of ancient fulachts: cracked stones in pits that may have been dug to reach water[5] (Ó Néill, 2003).

Taking all of this evidence we may perhaps tentatively conclude that the Fulacht na Morrigna was a type of multipurpose outdoor cooking pit. Meat would be cooked on spits, possibly on a rotating assembly or wheel, and water might be heated for use. The smaller fulachts were named for the Fíanna but the larger, and apparently more complex, fulachts were named for the Morrigan.

The Morrigan's fulacht is also associated with blacksmiths:

Perhaps because he also forges weapons of death, the blacksmith is sometimes thought to possess supernatural powers. As we have seen the author of an 8th century hymn asks God for protection from the spells of blacksmiths. The supernatural aspect of this craft is indicated further by the special treatment of the blacksmith in the list of professions in Bretha Nemed toísech. In the case of other craftsmen, three necessary skills are listed, but in the case of the blacksmith, the author draws on pagan mythology: 'three things which confer status on a blacksmith" the cooking spit of Nethin, the cooking pit of the Morrigan, the anvil of the Dagda. (Kelly, 2005, page 63)

It may be in this case that it is the skill to create these items which is the measure of the smith's worth, but it is uncertain.

End Notes

1 Book of Leinster version.
2 Literally the text says "bean derg" a red woman, however in Irish this is how hair color is usually given. See Audrey Nickel's "Color Me Irish" blog post for more on this. https://www.bitesize.irish/blog/color-me-irish/
3 For those who are interested in the use of color in Irish material it's given here as glas, or literally green, but green which can be anything from a light green or blue to a blue grey.
4 There are actually multiple words for the color red in Old Irish; I am using 'derg' here which is the one most often used in the texts to describe the Morrigans, et al, however it is not the only red used so that should be kept in mind.
5 It is worth noting here that O Néill concludes based on the date of the archaeological fulachts that they significantly predate the written accounts and therefore that the fulachts

were likely mere cooking pits; however, this leaves open the question of how evidence supports the pyrolithic use of fulachts and medieval texts also hint at this use if there is in actuality no connection.

Chapter 2

Misinformation and Truths About the Morrigan

The more popular the Morrigan becomes the more misinformation proliferates about her or connected to her, so let's focus here on clarifying some things. These aren't personal opinions but facts from the Irish language and mythology. Keep in mind, however, that everyone makes mistakes when it comes to things coming from other languages and everyone can fall prey to bad information being shared around, especially if they haven't read or aren't very familiar with the source material. So hopefully this chapter will help correct some of the most common mistakes and misinformation that is often floating around.

Is the Morrigan a Goddess?

One thing that I've seen repeated both online and in at least one book is the assertion that the Morrigan is never called a Goddess in Irish mythology or sources, so let's begin with that. The Morrigan is called a Goddess at least twice that I can think of offhand.

In the Metrical Dindshenchas, poem 49 Odras, which says:

> [then] the wife of the Dagda came,
> a phantom the shape-shifting Goddess.
> ...the mighty Mórrígan,
> whose ease was a host of troops.

In the Tochmarch Emire we also have this:

In the Wood of Badb, that is of the Morrigu, therefore her provenwood the land of Ross, and she is the Battle-Crow and is also called the woman of Neit, that is Goddess of Battle, because Neit is also a God of Battle.

Looking at the original language of each quote it is clear that the word used is in fact "goddess": día in the first example and bandee in the second. Gulermovich-Epstein in *War Goddess* also mentions that we have at least one prayer to the Morrigan, for success in a cattle raid, further cementing the view of her as a deity. I am not entirely sure where the idea began that she is never called one in the source material, but as you can see it is untrue.

How Do You Spell Her Name?

Another thing that I've been seeing off and on is people spelling the Morrigan's name 'Mhorrigan' or 'Mhorrigu'. Outside of some very specific circumstances[1] when writing in Irish the Morrigan's name is NOT spelled with an initial 'Mh'. Unless you are an Irish speaker writing in Irish in the case that calls for lenition, please don't do this. Its grammatically incorrect and it looks really weird. Also, it would then be pronounced Worrigan (or Vorrigan I suppose, depending on dialect). Which is how I read it every time I see it.

On a related note, there's also something of a trend to spell her name 'Morrighan'. I think this may be a version from the middle Irish that somehow mainstreamed, so it is a legitimate spelling. But as with the example above the pronunciation would be different, closer to 'MORE-ree-(gh)uhn', with the gh a sound that's swallowed at the back of the throat. The modern Irish is Mór-ríoghain, pronounced like 'MORE-ree-uhn' with the g lost entirely. If all of that looks like either too much effort or too hard to process then stick with the Anglicized Morrigan (MORE-rigann) or the Old Irish Morrigan (MORE-rih-gahn).

If this all seems like a huge pain in the butt, well, sorry, but this is the deal when you are honoring a goddess from a foreign culture and another language. Spelling matters. Pronunciation matters, in relation to the spelling you are using.

Why 'the' Morrigan?

Speaking of names, the Morrigan is always referred to with the definitive 'the' before her name, unless she's being directly addressed like in a prayer. I've been seeing a tendency for people to drop this recently, and it's worth keeping in mind that in Irish culture and mythology she's always referred to as *the* Morrigan. It may help to keep in mind that her name translates to a title – either Great Queen or Phantom Queen, so try thinking that you are saying that. Does it feel weird in English to say "I honor Great Queen" or "My goddess is Great Queen"? Which is why we say the Morrigan, the Great Queen.

Are Falcons Her Animal?

The idea that the Morrigan is associated with falcons and rebirth: not in the mythology or Irish folklore. I've traced this one back to an online article from 2005 which as far as I can tell is the source for the belief, as well as the idea that she is a Goddess of rebirth (also not something from mythology). The article was one person's thoughts and opinions and was not in any way based on mythology, but rather the person's intuition which the author was very upfront about.

The Morrigan and Cu Chulainn

This probably deserves a section of its own because of the amount of related misinformation, and in chapter 5 we will look in more depth at some retellings of their interactions during the Táin Bó Cúailnge. However here are some quick bullet points addressing the more common points:

The Morrigan loved Cu Chulainn: Well, no, not in a romantic way, not that we have any proof of although she certainly had an interest in him. There is one story (which does not appear in every version of the Táin Bó Cúailnge but only a few later ones) where she appears to him in disguise as a king's daughter, and she does tell him that she fell in love with him 'upon hearing of' his fame. However, this is highly suspicious for multiple reasons. Firstly, she's in disguise for a reason, because they two of them had previously met and had a rather dramatic disagreement with each other (see the Táin Bó Regamna). You would think if she really loved him, she'd show up as her Goddess-y self and offer that. Secondly, she's showing up at a point where he's already refused one king's daughter (Ailill and Medb's) and is filthy and starving. There's really nothing going on there to make anyone feel romantic. He tells her he's in a bad way and not in a position to meet a woman; she replies that she will help him; and he says he isn't guarding the ford to earn a woman's arse. At which point she threatens him. Now if she was actually in love with him, as a goddess of batt le, wouldn't she be pleased that he was putting honor and duty before pleasure? On the other hand, if the whole point was to trick him or anger him, she certainly achieves that.[2] She's also shown in her previous encounter with him in the Táin Bó Regamna that she's quite willing to lie to him as well as greatly annoy him, so this has much more of the feel of that to it than of any genuine profession of emotion.

The Morrigan offered Cu Chulainn sovereignty and he refused it or she denied it to him because he refused her: Again, from the same king's daughter story in the Táin Bó Cúailnge Let's be clear – she never offers him sovereignty. She also never offers to have sex with him, although that is implied by his responses.

What she actually says is that she has fallen in love with him because of his fame and that she has brought her treasures and her cattle. Nothing about making him a king or anything like that. Could someone argue it's implied? Perhaps, however Cu Chulainn was not a candidate for kingship which the Morrigan would have known. According to the Lebor Gabala Erenn it was Cu Chulainn who broke the Lia Fal[3] because it did not cry out under him or his foster son. And when the stone that cries out under the next king, the stone that is an Otherworldly treasure, is silent under someone they are really, really not sovereign material. I'd also quickly point out that when Irish Goddesses show up as Sovereignty to offer kingship to people, they generally do so disguised as withered old hags asking for a kiss or sex, to test the person's fitness to rule, not as gorgeous princesses offering their possessions.

The Morrigan and Cu Chulainn had sex or had a child: definitely not in the existing mythology.

What Exactly Happened with the Morrigan and Dagda That Samhain?

The Morrigan and the Dagda's union at Samhain is another thing I often hear misinformation about. If there is one story in Irish mythology relating to the Morrigan that most people are familiar with it is probably the scene in the Cath Maige Tuired where the Morrigan and the Dagda meet at a river, join, and then plan their strategy for the coming batt le with the Fomorians. There are several interpretations of this incident but possibly the most common are that it shows the Morrigan as a goddess of sex and that it is a case of the Dagda trading sex for victory. Basically, I hear people repeating the idea that the Dagda sought out the Morrigan before Samhain, before a big batt le, and had sex with her in exchange for her promise to help fight in the batt le and/or for batt le advice. I have a feeling the misinformation here is coming from people who haven't read the actual account or aren't very familiar with it but are only aware that the incident occurs.

This is a complicated one and is going to take a bit to untangle. First let's look at the actual story:

The Dagda had a house at Glenn Etin in the north. The Dagda was to meet a woman on a day, yearly, about Samain of the battle at Glen Etin. The Unish of Connacht calls by the south. The woman was at the Unish of Corand washing her genitals, one of her two feet by Allod Echae, that is Echumech, by water at the south, her other by Loscondoib, by water at the north. Nine plaits of hair undone upon her head. The Dagda speaks to her and they make a union. Laying down of the married couple was the name of that place from then. She is the Morrigan, the woman mentioned particularly here. Afterwards she commands[4] the Dagda to strip his land, that is Mag Scetne, against the Fomorians, and told the Dagda to call together the aes dana of Ireland to meet at the Ford of Unsen and she would go to Scetne and injure with magic the king of the Fomorians, that is Indech mac De Domnann is his name, and she would take the blood of his heart and kidneys of his battle-ardor from him. Because of that she will give to the gathered hosts the blood in her two palms, striking, groaning, warlike by the Ford of Unsen. Ford of Utter Destruction was its name afterwards because of the magical injury done to the king.
~ Cath Maige Tuired (translation mine)

Now it has been argued that she does this because he slept with her, in a sort of trade, but let's take a closer look at a few things. Firstly, this meeting is said to be *"dia bliadnae"* or on a day yearly, which implies that the two meet every year about that time. We have hints from other material that the Morrigan may be the Dagda's wife, specifically the Metrical Dindshenchas:

the wife of the Dagda
a phantom was the shapeshifting goddess
...the mighty Morrigan
whose ease is trooping hosts
Metrical Dindshenchas: Odras (translation mine)

One might note that the same word *"ben"* [wife/woman] is used in both the Dindshenchas and Cath Maige Tuired passages. Whether or not we give that any weight, we should at least consider that the two do have a connection outside this single story. So, we see a yearly meeting with two deities who are associated with each other outside of this story as well. They meet at a pre-arranged location where the Dagda finds the Morrigan straddling a river washing her genitals. The Dagda says something to her – about what we don't know. After making this union – giving the site its name of 'bed of the married couple' – the Morrigan tells the Dagda to strip his land, a common military ploy, in the place the Fomorians will be and to gather the armies of the Tuatha De Danann, and then promises to go out herself and destroy one of the Fomorian kings with magic, which she subsequently does, bringing back two handfuls of blood as proof. At no point does the story explicitly state that a deal is made between them, or that the Morrigan's actions are in any way a response to or payment for the Dagda's. We can say with certainty that she never makes an off er to him, although we do not know what he says to her when he first sees her.

My personal take on this is simple. The Dagda and the Morrigan meet every year and this particular year their meeting falls just before a major battle. After having sex, the Morrigan tells the Dagda exactly what he is to do and what she herself will be doing until he gathers the armies. Anyone who is married or in a long-term relationship should appreciate the interpersonal dynamics going on here.

Did the Morrigan grant her aid to the Tuatha De Danann in trade for the Dagda's attention? There's really no indication of that in the text. The Morrigan is a member of the Tuatha De Danann, daughter of Ernmas and Delbeath according to the Lebor Gabala Erenn, and had every reason to assist the Tuatha De without payment. We also need to keep in mind that before this meeting the Morrigan had already gone to Lugh and chanted a battle incitement to encourage him to rise up and fight, so she herself was clearly both in favor of the battle and already encouraging it and acting for the Tuatha De.

It's an interesting passage and full of important information about both Gods, but I think we need to be cautious in rushing to interpret it, especially through a modern lens. Instead, I think we need to look at what's actually going on and being said, and what happens, and let the story speak for itself.

To summarize:

- The Dagda didn't seek her out, it was a yearly pre-arranged meeting at that location.
- We have no idea what they discussed before having sex, only that they talked.
- Yes, they had sex, but according to the Dindshenchas they were married, and also in the text of the Cath Maige Tuired where we find this particular story it refers to the location this happened at as 'the bed of the married couple'. I realize most translations give it as Bed of the Couple but the exact word used, Lanamhou, is a version of a term for one of the legal states of marriage in Irish law.
- Yes, the Morrigan did give the Dagda battle advice right after the sex and did aid the Tuatha De Danann by promising to weaken one of the opposing kings, but she

had already been aiding them, specifically by singing an incitement to Lugh to encourage him to fight and prepare for the battle. Since she'd already acted on her own to help them before this it doesn't make sense to see this meeting between a married couple at a yearly tryst as some kind of pay-off for her to help her own people.

Basically, what we have is a yearly meeting of a married couple at a specific location, some marital sex, some martial advice, and some batt le magic against a common enemy.

This is just touching on a handful of the most common bits of misinformation or errors that I tend to see. There are sure to be more, of course, and in the next chapter we will take a deep dive into the Morrigan's confusion with two other goddesses. I hope this helped to clear some things up.

End Notes

1 For example in the vocative case, but that doesn't apply in the vast majority of cases where I've seen people using this spelling in English.

2 There's also been some supposition by scholars that this entire scene was added later to explain her coming at him in three animal forms in the next scene, for those unfamiliar with her promise to do so in the Táin Bó Regamna. It is certainly odd that she threatens to do so in the TBR, then appears as Buan's daughter in the TBC only to make the exact same threat again, however, this would make sense if it were a case of scribes duplicating a scene or trying to re-explain something, or even integrating material from a different oral source (all things that aren't uncommon).

3 After it didn't cry out under him Cu Chulainn struck the stone and it has remained silent ever since.

4   I'm translating itbert, which is a form of as-beir, as
    commands, although it has nuanced meanings. It can mean
    says or speaks, but in a sense of orders which I believe is
    what the Morrigan is giving here it means commands. It can
    also mean singing or chanting.

Chapter 3

Nemain and Morgen la Fey: Untangling Confusing Connections

It's impossible to discuss the Morrigan without also discussing a variety of other beings who are connected to Her. In *Pagan Portals – the Morrigan* I tried to do this by discussing the other goddesses who are often called Morrigan or conflated with the Morrigan. There are a couple however where the confusion runs particularly deep and is so often perpetuated in modern material that the older sources are buried or ignored. What I'd like to do here, as we continue our journey to know the Morrigan on a deeper level, is dig into two of the beings most often confused with the Morrigan herself and look at why that happens and also why we should be cautious about that line of thought.

Nemain, Goddess of War

If you ask most Celtic pagans to name the three Morrigans a good number of them, in my experience, will say Badb, Macha, and Nemain despite the fact that Nemain is never explicitly called the Morrigan or included with the other two anywhere in Irish mythology. I personally blame this one on the multitude of modern pagan books which blithely say that the above-named trio are the three Morrigans, however it can likely be traced back to Hennessey's 1870 book *The Ancient Irish Goddess of War*. Hennessey put a lot of emphasis on Nemain and included her with Badb and Macha in his discussion of the Morrigan in a way that I feel led to the later conflation of Nemain with the three daughters of Ernmas elsewhere called the three Morrigans.

The primary source we have for Nemain in mythology is the Táin Bó Cúailnge (TBC) and this is often the main evidence people point to in support of Nemain as one of the Morrigan.

The TBC material is pretty thin though and just shows her acting as a war Goddess, alone or with Badb. At one point in the story Cu Chulainn shouts and arouses the supernatural forces, after which Nemain appears: "*Co ro mesc ind Neamain (.i. in Badb) forsin t-slóg.*" (Windisch, 1905). [So that Nemain, that is the Badb, intoxicated the army there]. The equating of Nemain and Badb is common and can be found in multiple sources where the two names are treated as interchangeable, although as we shall see the two also appear together fairly often. In another recension of the TBC we see Nemain appearing with Badb and Be Neit, shrieking and terrifying the gathered army. Heijda suggests – and I agree – that is quite likely that instead of "*Badb 7 Be Neit 7 Nemain*" [Badb and Be Neit and Nemain] this passage should read "*Badb .i. Be Neit 7 Nemain*" [Badb that is Be Neit and Nemain] (Heijda, 2007). This is entirely logical as Be Neit rarely appears anywhere as an individual being and in the glossaries is usually equated with either Badb or the Morrigan, and sometimes Nemain. In point of fact the name Be Neit simply means woman or wife of battle and may be a general term used to describe war Goddesses rather than a proper name, which would also explain why in glossary entries she is so often immediately equated to another named deity. Towards the end of the TBC we see Nemain appearing alone in a similar occurrence:

> *...so that Nemain brought intoxication upon the army there, falling*
> *in their armor and on the points of their spears and sword-edges, so*
> *a hundred warriors of them die in the midst of the encampment and*
> *at the side of that place a time of terror the cry carried from on high.*

Windisch, 1905, translation mine).

This may be a repeat of the same behavior by Nemain, which would support her role as a war Goddess who brings terror and madness, but in fairness it could also be a scribal error where the same incident was doubled. In any event it is safe to say that in the TBC Nemain is associated with a cry which causes terror in those who hear it, and brings such panic that people fall on their own weapons or kill their comrades.

Heijda favors the idea of Nemain as an alternate name for Badb or as a goddess paired with Badb separate from the Morrigan. In the Lebor Gabala Erenn we are told that Badb and Nemain are two wives of Net: "*Net son of Indui, his two wives, Badb and Nemain without falsehood* ". In another version we are told that it is Fea and Nemain who are his wives and that they are sisters, daughters of Elcmar: "*Fea and Nemain: two wives of Net son of Indui, that is two daughters of Elcmar of the Brugh*". Due to this Heijda suggests that Fea may be the name of Badb in the same way that Anand is for Morrigu (Heijda, 2007). Macalister agrees, suggesting that Fea and Nemain represent an earlier twin-pairing which evolved into the grouping of Badb and Nemain; he also suggests that Badb became a dyad with the Morrigu before becoming a triplicity with Morrigu and Macha (Macalister, 1940). This would suggest an interesting evolution for Badb as a primary war Goddess who formed a pairing with her sister Nemain, who she shares a father with, in some areas and with her two sisters, Morrigu and Macha, who she shares a mother with, elsewhere.

In contrast, Gulermovich-Epstein prefers to see Nemain as one of the Morrigan although indirectly connected. This argument uses several degrees of separation in different glossaries to connect the Morrigan to Nemain. An entry in Cormac's Glossary says Nemain is Net's wife and also called Be Neit – "*Net that is a God of battle. Nemain his wife. She is*

Be Neit". There are several versions of this, but all are fairly homogenous. Since Badb and the Morrigan are also called Be Neit elsewhere Gulermovich-Epstein argues that Nemain may be one of the Morrigan (Gulermovich-Epstein, 1998). Of course, this is highly problematic in that "Be Neit" may not be a name at all and could just mean "woman of battle" and as such could be applied to any war Goddess. There is an entry in O'Clery's Glossary *"Nemhain that is crow of battle* [literally badb catha] *or a hooded crow"* (Gulermovich-Epstein, 1998). But O'Clery is extremely late – 17th century – and it's hard to say at that point if his statement that Nemain was Badb is a corruption of earlier beliefs or legitimate, and also since "badb catha" isn't capitalized at all it is possible he didn't mean it as a name at all but was simply calling her *"a crow of battle"* as he follows it with *"or a hooded crow"*.

O'Clery's Glossary also gives us *"Nemain, that is madness or insanity[1]"* Gulermovich-Epstein, 1998). Another entry in Cormac's Glossary gives us: *"Be Neit, that is Neit the name of the man. The woman Nemain his wife. They are a poisonous couple indeed"*. In O'Mulconry's Glossary we are told: *"Red Nemain, that is heat of a fire, that is: red Nemain passion and the rest"*. It is interesting that O'Mulconry associates Nemain with both fire and passion, adding a layer of depth to her usual associations. It is also quite interesting that he calls her *"Nemain derga"* – red Nemain – as this is a common name given to Badb who is called the red Badb and the red-mouthed Badb. Additionally, we know that Nemain was a magic worker for the Tuatha De Danann, listed with the other war goddesses: *"Nemain, Danand, Badb and Macha, Morrigu who brings victory, impetuous and swift Etain, Be Chuilli of the north country, were the sorceresses of the Tuatha De."* (Banshenchus, n.d.)

Another fascinating tidbit about Nemain's character can be gleaned from a passage of the Lebor Gabala Erenn which is discussing several women of the Tuatha De Danann, including the two sovereignty goddesses, Banba and Fotla, Danann, the three Morrigans – Macha, Badb, and Morrigu – and Fea and Nemain:

Banba, Fotla and Fea,
Nemain wise in poetry,
Danand mother of the Gods.
Badb and Macha rich in wealth
Morrigan powerful in sorcery
They encompass iron-death battles
the daughters of Ernmas.

Overall, it seems clear she was associated Badb and Fea and was called both Badb and Be Neit herself. She does often appear acting with Badb though, suggesting that when she is called Badb it is being used as a title, rather than that she herself is Badb. We know she was one of the sorceresses of the Tuatha De Danann and also that she was said to be wise in poetry and *"without falsehood"*, and Cormac's Glossary calls her poisonous. When we see her appearing in stories in an active role, she is a bringer of *"mesc"*, that is drunkenness, intoxication, and confusion which is directly associated with her terrifying cry. She is madness, insanity, frenzy, and perhaps the passion of batt le. Whether or not she was one of the Morrigan, per se, she was without doubt a Goddess of war and batt le, and strongly associated with Badb. It does seem likely when looking at the total of the gathered material that Nemain originally formed a war Goddess pair with Badb, as the two are often associated with each other and act together, and Nemain is given the title of Badb. Certainly, she has been considered one of the Morrigan grouping for centuries now and deserves a portion of the title in a modern sense, if only as one of the great Irish war Goddesses.

Why Is Macha Included as One of the Morrigans and Not Nemain?

Because of the modern confusion around Nemain and the regular inclusion of Nemain along with Badb and the Morrigan there is sometimes confusion about why Macha is included among the three Morrigan and Nemain isn't. I hope in the first section of this chapter we've covered why Nemain isn't the Morrigan and wasn't historically viewed as one of the three Morrigans. But because the question around Macha and Nemain is persistent today let's take a look at that as well.

The simple answer is that we know Macha is one of the three Morrigan because she is referred to explicitly as such in several of the glossaries and we know Nemain isn't because she is at no point in the source material called the Morrigan or one of the Morrigans.

The complicated answer is that while Macha's connection to the Morrigan is easy to establish and fairly clear – she is repeatedly referred to as one of the three daughters of Ernmas with the Morrigan and Badb, is listed as one of the three Morrigans with the same two sisters, and acts along with them in stories – Nemain's connection is more convoluted as we just discussed. We can clearly say that she is a war and battle goddess and that she acts in ways that are similar to what we see the Morrigan doing. She is also very closely tied to Badb, who is one of the Morrigan.

Badb and Nemain share similar epithets including 'red' and 'red mouthed' and Nemain is sometimes referred to as 'Nemain, that is the Badb' or 'Nemain that is the Badb Catha'. It is likely that Badb's name like the Morrigan is also a title but in this case, we can see the use of it applied to Nemain indicating their close ties to each other. Nemain is also referred to as Be Neit which may mean wife of Net[2] or woman of battle and is itself a name or title we see applied to other war goddesses. Nemain is said to be the wife of Net along with Badb in some sources, while others say she is his wife along with her sister Fea; unlike the three daughters of Ernmas Fea and Nemain are daughters of Elcmar. This is not a clear subject however, with some scholars like Heijda favoring the idea that Nemain is Badb's true name, while others like Gulermovich-Epstein seeing Nemain as one of the multitude of Morrigan goddesses but indirectly connected.

We can say with certainty that she is not one of the three if we are looking specifically at that triple grouping, but we can also say that she does appear together with Badb inciting battle and causing strife. While we can confidently include her among Irish war goddesses whether or not she is one of the Morrigan per se will probably always be an open question. On the other hand, Macha's place among the Morrigan is strongly established in the source material.

The Morrigan and Morgen la Fey

One source of much confusion is the connection – or lack thereof – between the Irish goddess the Morrigan and the Welsh Arthurian figure Morgen le Fay.[3] This is a subject that has been muddled in modern paganism for a long time and I won't deny that there are plenty of books out there that will directly contradict what I am about to say. People are very drawn to the idea that these two goddesses are connected or are the same being and it is an idea that many people are reluctant to reconsider. That said I am presenting here the source material and research I found when I investigated the potential historic connection between the two.

The short answer is historically there's no connection between the Morrigan and Morgen le Fay.

The Morrigan is an Irish goddess with complex associations to battle, war, death, prophecy, sovereignty, magic, incitement, and victory. Her name in older forms of Irish was pronounced roughly 'MORE-rih-guhn' and later forms 'MORE-ree-uhn' and meant either great queen or phantom queen, depending what etymology one favors. We have a wide selection of mythology and folklore featuring her and it's clear that when she shows up, she's an active force in whatever she's doing.

The Morrigan has two sisters, Badb and Macha, who she appears with in some myths usually performing battle magic; in the Táin Bó Cúailnge she also appears with Nemain and Be Neit for the same purpose. The Morrigan in later mythology would come to be associated with night terrors and specters, viewed as demonic because she could not easily be turned into a meek saint.

Morgen le Fay is a character first found in Arthurian stories, Specifically, the 12th century works of Geoffrey of Monmouth, where her name was initially spelled Morgen le Fay. It is worth noting that this spelling is significant because while both Morgan and Morgen are men's names (also worth noting) they are pronounced differently – Morgan evolved into the modern Welsh Morcant while Morgen became Morien (Jones, 1997). In the 12th century Morgen would have been pronounced, roughly, 'Mor-YEN' (Jones, 1997). The name Morgen is generally believed to mean 'sea born'.

Geoffrey was collecting local stories from Wales and publishing them in France and while he certainly didn't invent Morgen for his Viti Merlini there is no way to know for certain how much, or little, he shaped the character as he preserved her. Which in fairness is true for all of the Arthurian characters he wrote about. That aside however Geoffrey's Morgen was a priestess, one of nine sisters connected to Avalon. In the 15th century Morgen would be renamed Morgan by Thomas Malory and recast as King Arthur's scheming half-sister who was set against both Arthur and his wife Guinevere.

One of the main arguments connecting the names is that they sound the same to modern English speakers, but I hope it's clear here that in Irish and Welsh the two names sound very different. They also have different meanings and that is significant. Another argument that favors them being the same deity is that they are both connected to magic, but while one may argue that both do, indeed, practice enchantment, the nature of the magic they practice seems to be vitally different and outside of that single similarity the rest of their associations are very different. Morgen is connected to healing and, perhaps, to guiding the dead or dying to Avalon or the Otherworld; the Morrigan is associated with death and battle but nothing in her mythology relates her to healing or to a role as a psychopomp[4]. People also argue that their stories have similar themes, but this is clearly not so. The Morrigan is married to the Dagda and may or may not try to seduce Cu Chulainn in one story while Morgen in various stories is married, is adulterous, and even tricks her own brother into conceiving a son with her. The Morrigan incites battles by directly encouraging people to rise up and fight while Morgen, in some of her stories, sows discord in more subtle ways. The Morrigan's main location is a cave, Uaimh na gCat, while Morgen's is an island on a lake, Avalon. These are only a few examples just to illustrate the very different natures of the two beings.

The Morrigan and Morgen le Fay are often associated with each other in modern paganism, perhaps because they are both perceived as powerful and potentially dangerous women who have gotten a bad reputation that they may not deserve. Both certainly, were vilified and demonized over time as stories evolved, the Morrigan going from a goddess to a night specter and Morgen from a priestess of Avalon to an incestuous and usurping sister of the king. I certainly understand why people see associations between the two, although for myself I'd be more likely to picture them sharing stories at the bar over shots together than to believe they are the same being or energy.

I am aware of theories that Morgen was originally a Welsh goddess; I cannot say whether or not Morgen is a deity or ever was a deity, nor do I deny that someone does answer when people call on Morgen le Fay today. What I can say is that there's no evidence that the Morrigan and Morgen le Fay share any roots or that historically the two have any connection to each other.

End Notes

1 Dásach is a term which can mean fury, frenzy, violence; the related word dásacht is applied to rabid animals, but it can also mean ecstasy or war-like rage. It carries implications of a sudden uncontrolled fit of emotion.

míre is a form of mer and means demented, crazy, rash, but can also be used in a positive sense to mean spirited or lively. It would be equally accurate to translate this passage as "Nemain, that is fury or terror" however I feel my translation uses the two words in a synonymous sense which seems to have been the intent of the original.

2 Net is an obscure war god.

3 I am aware that in modern terms her name is often given now as Morgan la Fey, however, I am choosing to go with the older original spelling used by the first person to write her name down.

4 See Chapter 4 for discussion of modern myth relating to the Morrigan's connection to psychopomp activities and rebirth.

Chapter 4

The Morrigan's Role in the Cath Maige Tuired[1]

A key text of Irish mythology is the Cath Maige Tuired, a tale of war between the Tuatha De Danann and the Fomorians over the right to rule Ireland. One particular figure who appears repeatedly throughout the story is the Irish war goddess the Morrigan, yet her role in the text is often difficult to fully understand using existing English translations which omit significant amounts of her dialogue and, due to translation choices, in some cases give an imprecise impression of her actions. When the Cath Maige Tuired is looked at in full in the original language the Morrigan's role within the story takes on greater significance and nuances, which are otherwise lost, become clear. Taking each of her appearances in turn, with more literal translations, will show the importance of her actions in inciting the batt le, using magic to fight against the Fomorians, and rallying the Tuatha De Danann to victory before finally offering a dual prophecy of the fate of the people to come.

To begin it must be understood that the Cath Maige Tuired (CMT) itself presents a challenge to translators, resulting in the current popular translations by Elizabeth Gray and Whitley Stokes both omitting passages, some of them lengthy. In a 2014 lecture by John Carey called "A London Library, An Irish Manuscript, A British Myth? The Wanderings of 'The Battle of Moytirra'" Carey traces the history of the only extant manuscript containing this vital Irish myth and discusses the unique difficulties it presents. One of the most important points in Carey's lecture is that the manuscript for the Cath Maige Tuired is believed by scholars to have been written by a younger scribe who was fond of intentionally obscuring his writing with:

...willfully eccentric orthography in which certain aspects of Old Irish, together with other usages which seem to be the fruits of pure fantasy, are deployed without rhyme or reason to produce a kind of Irish which looks like nothing else on earth. (Carey, 2014, p 8).

What this means in practical terms is that the Irish of the CMT is non-standard and sometimes impossible to fully relate to known words in either Old or Middle Irish. There are points where it is difficult to be sure what a word is supposed to be and others where it is left entirely to supposition. Perhaps this is why Stokes chose, even in the Irish, to omit passages entirely; Gray included the full Irish text however chose not to translate all of it. For my purposes here I have included my own translations of passages often omitted or not fully translated as they are pertinent to the Morrigan's role in the story; however expert linguists don't agree on what some of these words are so my translations should be understood as educated guesses and may be open to further interpretation[2].

Warfare for the Irish was a highly ritualized and structured affair and poetic incitement before battle was an established practice (Gulermovich Epstein, 1998). This incitement served to both demoralize the enemy and to inspire one's own side; in the Irish material this is manifested as laíded, incitement through inspirational speech, and gressacht, incitement through derogatory speech or insults (MacCana, 1992). The importance of such incitement, and its role in battle, cannot be understated. Both laíded and gressacht acted as essential forerunners to actual battle, ensuring that the individual or army was sufficiently motivated to fight to victory. Perhaps related to both of these are rosc catha, magical battle chants, which are also employed and, in many cases, may be identical to laíde in stories. The effect of the rosc catha and laíded in the stories are magical in nature but also appear to have a psychological aspect, in that they provide confidence and courage to the army being supported by them.

The first appearance of the Morrigan occurs after Lugh has been accepted at Tara and initial plans for the battle against the Fomorians have begun. The Tuatha De Danann have separated for three years to prepare for the coming fight. The Morrigan goes to Lugh and incites him to battle, using a laíded as follows.[3]

Undertake a battle of overthrowing," so to the Gods sang the Morrigan turning to Lug, "Awake, make a hard slaughter, smiting bodies, attacks boiling, greatly burning, devastating, the people to a man crying out...

Looking at the full passage in Irish we see that the Morrigan is not merely urging Lugh to "awake" but to fight fiercely and mercilessly against the Fomorians. The intense tone seems meant to inspire and motivate him to equally strong action. Such an approach is typical of laíded, a practice which Proinsias MacCana likens to psychological warfare and can involve either demoralizing one's enemy or invigorating one's own forces (MacCana, 1992). It is important to note as well that this passage occurs directly after Lugh, accompanied by two champions of the Tuatha De Danann, the Dagda and Ogma, has gone to the three Gods of skill and been equipped with arms and armor specially prepared for the war and immediately before Firgol the druid gave a prophesy of the batt le to strengthen the resolve of the Tuatha De Danann. This series of events could also fi t with the ritualized approach to conflict to which the laíded could belong (MacCana, 1992). We see the Morrigan initially within this context as a force of incitement, setting things in motion and inspiring battle.

After Firgol's prophecy the Morrigan reappears, this time in a short passage where she is meeting the Dagda, relaying battle strategy, and magically attacking the Fomorian king Indech:

The Dagda had a house at Glenn Etin in the north. The Dagda was to meet a woman on a day, yearly, about Samain of the battle at Glen Etin. The Unish of Connacht calls by the south. The woman
was at the Unish of Corand washing her genitals, one of her two feet
by Allod Echae, that is Echumech, by water at the south, her other
by Loscondoib, by water at the north. Nine plaits of hair undone upon her head. The Dagda speaks to her and they make a union. Laying Down of the Married Couple was the name of that place from then. She is the Morrigan, the woman mentioned particularly
here.
Afterwards she commands the Dagda to strip his land, that is Mag Scetne, against the Fomorians, and told the Dagda to call together the aes dana of Ireland to meet at the Ford of Unsen and she would go to Scetne and injure with magic the king of the Fomorians, that is Indech mac De Domnann is his name, and she would take the blood of his heart and kidneys of his battle-ardor from him. Because of that she will give to the gathered hosts the blood in her two palms, striking, groaning, warlike by the Ford of Unsen. Ford of Utter Destruction was its name afterwards because
of the magical injury done to the king.

This meeting is interesting in several ways. Firstly, this meeting is said to be *"dia bliadnae"* or on a day yearly, which implies that the two meet every year about that time. We have hints from other material that the Morrigan may be the Dagda's wife, specifically the Metrical Dindshenchas:

the wife of the Dagda
a phantom was the shape-shifting goddess
...the mighty Morrigan
whose ease is trooping hosts.

One might note that the same word *"ben"* is used in both the Dindshenchas and Cath Maige Tuired passages. Also, within this section of text in the CMT the term *"lanomhnou"* is used, which appears to be a variant of lánamna the genitive singular of lánamain which means married couple. Whether or not any weight is given to this, it is worth considering that the two do have a connection outside this single story. They meet at a pre-arraigned location where the Dagda finds the Morrigan straddling a river washing her genitals. The Dagda says something to her, but what is unknown. The two then make a union and the Morrigan tells the Dagda to strip his land, a common military ploy, in the place the Fomorians will be and to gather the armies of the Tuatha De Danann. She then promises to go out herself and destroy one of the Fomorian kings with magic, which she subsequently does, bringing back two handfuls of blood as proof. This action as described in the text involves the Morrigan going to the gathered army of the Tuatha De Danann with two palmfuls of blood which she then strikes while groaning. The word used, oconn, is also a term occasionally used for incitement, although much less frequently then laíded or gressacht. It is possible that a more accurate translation of that sentence might be *"Because of that she will give to the gathered hosts the blood in her two palms, striking, inciting, warlike by the Ford of Unsen."* If this is so then this is the second occurrence of the Morrigan actively inciting the army to batt le, which as will become apparent may be one of her strongest themes in this story. Certainly, whether it is active incitement or inspiration through action her magical destruction of Indech and her public presentation of his blood to the army is meant to encourage her own side to victory.

The next appearance of the Morrigan is just prior to the battle, when Lugh questions the gathered Tuatha De Danann about what they will contribute to the fight:

> *"And you, oh Morrigan," said Lugh, "what ability?"*
> *"Not hard," said she, "Pursue what was observed, pursue to strike down, I control bloody destruction."*

Here the Morrigan, as in her promise to the Dagda to destroy Indech, is boldly proclaiming her own abilities. Although the word *"ar-rosdibu"* is cryptic if it is taken as an atypical compound word and broken down into ar ros dibu the meaning could be given as "bloody destruction" which is perhaps intended to echo her earlier delivery of Indech's blood to the hosts. In that case it becomes both a play on words and also a reminder of her previous attack on the Fomorian king. In this passage, unlike the others, there is no discernible battle incitement but the proclamation of her own prowess and dominion over that which she pursues is clear.

The two sides engage each other and the battle is not going in favor of the Tuatha De Danann. It is at this point that the Morrigan re-enters the story once again to incite the army, this time to turn the tide of battle and ensure victory.

Once again Stokes and Gray avoid the bulk of this material. Gray gives it simply as:

Then the Morrigan the daughter of Ernmas came, and she was strengthening the Tuatha De to fight the battle resolutely and fiercely. She then chanted the following poem: "Kings arise to the battle! (Gray, 1983).

Similarly, Stokes offers it as:

Then the Morrígan, daughter of Ernmass, came, and was heartening the Tuatha Dea to fight the battle fiercely and fervently. So then she sang this lay below: 'Kings arise to the battle', etc. (Stokes, 1891).

This is unfortunate because while the language is difficult and obscure it is evocative. My own translation:

Next the Morrigan daughter of Ernmas came, and urged the Tuatha De Danann to give battle stubbornly and savagely. So that in that place she chanted her incitement down: "Arise, kings to battle here! Seizing honor, speaking battle-spells, destroying flesh, flaying, snaring, seizing battle — seeking out forts, giving out a death feast, fighting battles, singing poems, proclaiming druids collect tribute around in memory. Bodies wounded in a rushing assault, pursuing, exhausting, breaking, prisoners taken, destruction blooms, hearing screams, fostering armies battle, occupants moving, a boat sails, arsenal cuts off noses. I see the birth of every bloody battle, redwombed, fierce, obligatory-battlefield, enraged. Against the point of a sword, reddened shame, without-great-battlements, preparing towards them, proclaiming a line of battle Fomorians in the chanted margins, helpfully impels a reddened vigorous champion, shaking hound-killing warriors together, bloody beating, ancient warband towards their doom.

As with her earlier incitement of Lugh, the full text makes it plain that the Morrigan is not merely urging the kings to "arise to battle" but rather to arise and fight to the destruction of their enemies. This is clearly a type of laíded and indeed while the verb used is rocachain, a form of canaid, "sing or chant", the noun is "laíd-se" which in context I am translating as "her incitement". When laíded are used in other material, such as the Táin Bó Cuailnge, they normally occur with the verb form (MacCana, 1992). This may be a way to emphasize to the audience that incitement is occurring before the actual poetic speech is presented, and in this case the use of the noun form of the word could be another play on words. Her goal of incitement is achieved as her words spur the Tuatha De Danann to turn the tide of batt le and achieve victory.

Several small incidents occur at the end of the battle including the now-deposed king Bres bargaining with Lugh for his life and the Dagda pursuing his harper who has been taken by the retreating Fomorians. The Morrigan's final appearance, indeed the end of the story as we have it, occurs after the carnage has been cleared away when the gathered Tuatha De Danann call on the Morrigan and ask if she has any news and she replies with two poems. The first is a prophecy of peace.

Although this prophecy is one of the most well-known of the Morrigan's dialogues, Gray translates only the first eight lines and Stokes only the first four. Both found the remaining text too obscure to attempt to translate, with Stokes ending the fourth line with "etc.," and Gray inserting "gap; meaning of text unclear" (Stokes, 1891; Gray, 1983). The following is my own understanding of the full poem:

After the defeat at the battle's end and the clearing out of the carnage, the Morrigan daughter of Ernmas arrived to announce the deaths of the battle there, and the mighty victory done there to the fair knights of Ireland and beings of fairy-swords, and beings of proud waters, and beings of abounding rivermouths. Thus, that Badb recounts great exploits still. "Have you any story?" They all turned towards her there mentioned before.

"Peace to sky.

Sky to earth.

Earth below sky,

strength in each one,

a cup overfull,

filled with honey,

sufficiency of renown.

Summer in winter,

spears supported by warriors,

warriors supported by forts.

Forts fiercely strong;

banished are sad outcries

land of sheep

healthy under antler-points

destructive battle cries held back.

Crops [masts] on trees

a branch resting

resting with produce

sufficiency of sons

a son under patronage

on the neck of a bull

a bull of magical poetry

knots in trees

trees for fire.

Fire when wished for.

Wished for earth

getting a boast

proclaiming of borders.

Borders declaring prosperity

green-growth after spring
autumn increase of horses
a troop for the land
land that goes in strength and abundance.
Be it a strong, beautiful wood, long-lasting a great boundary
'Have you a story?'
Peace to sky
be it so lasting to the ninth generation

This prophecy of peace is followed immediately by a second prophecy, with a much grimmer tone:

She was afterwards among them prophesying the years at the end of existence, and further promising each evil and lack in those years, and every plague and every vengeance: so that there she chanted her poem:

Something seen is a world that shall not be pleasing: summer deprived of flowers, cows deprived of milk; women deprived of modesty, men deprived of valor. Conquests without a king, pointed, bearded, mouths of many-oaths, sorrow, a lord without judgments. Sea without profit. Multitude of storms, excessively tonsured, forts, barren of structures, hollow, a stronghold coming from mistakes a devastated time, many homeless, an excess of lords, joy in evil, a cry against traditions, bearded faces. Equipment decaying, numerous exploits, finding battles, silent towards a spurred horse, numerous assemblies, treachery of lord's sons, covered in sorrow, crooked judgement of old men. False precedents of judges, a betrayer every man. A reaver every son. The son will go lay down instead of his father. The father will go lay down instead of his son. In-law each to his own kinsman. A person will not seek women out of his house. A long enduring evil period of time will be generated, a son betrays his father, a daughter betrays [her mother][4]

Looking at the two poems together provides insight not only into the Morrigan as a prophetess but also demonstrates basic features of what the Irish at the time considered good and bad conditions to live in. In the first prophecy peace is all encompassing, extending from sky to earth and the world is full of plenty in all ways. Borders are strong and secure, sad cries and batt le cries are gone, and the land has strength and abundance. In contrast the second prophecy offers a vision of the exact opposite: lack in all important areas, discontent and dishonor, false judgements, and rampant incest. Unfortunately, the manuscript ends abruptly in mid-sentence, making it impossible to guess how the prophecy would have ended.

The Cath Maige Tuired is an important mythological text which provides a great deal of information about the Irish gods and their early time in Ireland. One of the most significant of these gods is the Morrigan who plays an essential role in the rebellion against the Fomorians using both her own magical power and the poetic form of laíded. The Morrigan repeatedly appears in the story to incite the Tuatha De Danann to battle with obvious good effect. These acts of incitement all occur at pivotal points where her involvement seems crucial to ensuring victory: she appears to incite Lugh to fight after he is armed, she appears to the gathered army *"groaning, warlike"* after a pledge to destroy the Fomorian King Indech, and finally she appears at the turning point of the battle to incite the Tuatha De Danann to rise up and claim victory. In each case her incitement is strongly worded, direct, and relentless. She promises to use magic to injure the Fomorian king Indech by taking his battle ardor, bring back two handfuls of his blood to the gathered army, and Indech is later overcome and killed in the final battle, almost certainly as a result of the Morrigan's battle magic. At the end she prophecies a positive and negative fate for the world, having ensured victory for her own side. Looking carefully at the Irish text and literal translations of the text it becomes plain that the Morrigan is a driving force in the battle, both through incitement and active participation. It is perhaps fitting that the extant text ends with the Morrigan's words of prophecy, as she played a vital role in instigating and ensuring the outcome.

End Notes

1 This section was originally published as an article titled 'The Role of the Morrigan in the Cath Maige Tuired: Incitement, Battle Magic and Prophecy' in Air n-Aithesc vol. II, issue II, August 2015. What appears here is a modified and edited version.

2 Isolde Carmody of Story Archeology has also given versions of some of these which can be found here: https:// storyarchaeology.com/the-morrigan-speaks-her-threepoems-2/ I encourage people to read the different versions to compare them, as this can help give a better understanding of the overall feel of the material.

3 This passage is particularly difficult to translate, and neither Stokes nor Gray give a full version of it. This may be understandable as the text following the initial sentence is difficult and presents issues typical of the problems endemic in the CMT, however what I am offering here is my own understanding of the passage.

4 The existing manuscript of the Cath Maige Tuired ends with the line 'a son betrays his father, a daughter betrays' but it seems logical to extrapolate that the sentence would finish 'her mother' if we had the following page.

Chapter 5

Re-telling the Ulster Cycle: The Morrigan and Cu Chulainn

There is possibly no subject relating to the Morrigan that causes more confusion or contention than that of the relationship between the Morrigan and Cu Chulainn. In the modern pagan community new myths and stories are growing relating to these two and new approaches to understanding them; I am not trying to tell anyone what to believe here. What I do want to do however is clarify what the older source material has to say because I understand that not everyone reads this material directly themselves or is familiar with the older stories.

For those who haven't read the Ulster Cycle consider this a slightly abridged re-telling of the Morrigan's interactions with Cu Chulainn, beginning with the encounter that sets up their encounters in the Táin Bó Cuailgne. These section focuses on the incidents in these stories where the Morrigan and Cu Chulainn interact to show the nature of their relationship across its course; however, I am not including every single interaction they have across all mythology, rather I am focusing on the Táin Bó Cúailnge, one rémscel [pre-tale] the Táin Bó Regamna, and the Aided Cu Chulainn.

In the Táin Bó Regamna

Cu Chulainn wakes up to the sound of a cow bellowing. Leaping out of bed naked he runs outside with his wife Emer chasing him carrying his clothes. He yells to his charioteer, Laeg, to ready their chariot and they go to find out what all the hubbub is about. After a short ride they come upon a strange sight: a chariot pulled by a one-legged red horse, with the chariot post affixed through the horse's body and forehead. In the chariot is a red-haired woman wearing a red cloak which trails to the ground; next to it is a large man using a hazel rod to drive a cow who is bellowing.

Cu Chulainn points out that the cow doesn't like the way she's being driven and the woman replies that its none of his business because it's not his cow, or his friend's cow. Cu Chulainn then says that it is his business because every cow in Ulster is his business, to which the woman replies that he takes on a lot. He then asks why she is talking to him and the man isn't and she says because she's the one he yelled at. He then says that when she speaks, she speaks for the man and she replies by giving the man's name as "Cold wind-conflict-brightness-strife".

Cu Chulainn remarks that this is a wondrous name and asks if she is going to speak for him the whole time and what her name is, at which point the man speaks, and tells him that the woman's name is "Keen edged-small lipped-plain cloaked-hair-sharp shouting-fierceness-a phantom".

Cu Chulainn gets angry at this point and accuses them of trying to make a fool of him, then leaps onto the woman in the chariot and holds a spear to her head, asking her who she really is.

She tells him that she is a satirist and that the cow was payment for a poem, given to her by Daire mac Fiachnai of Cúailnge So, Cu Chulainn says that he wants to hear her recite a poem and she says she will if he will get off of her, which he does, jumping down between the chariot poles.

She proceeds to recite a poem against him and he leaps into his own chariot only to find that the woman, cow, and man have disappeared and only a black bird remains perched in a tree nearby.

He calls her a hurtful woman and she says that the place they are at will be named 'Bog of Distress' because of his words.

He says if he knew who he was talking to they wouldn't have parted that way and she pledges that whatever he would have done it would still have ended badly for him. He then says that she has no power over him, to which she replies that she does indeed, and that she is bringing and will bring his death; she then explains that she has brought the cow from out of the Sidhe of Cruachan to be bred by the Brown Bull of Cúailnge and that the calf it carries will start a great cattle raid, and implies that Cu Chulainn will die in this raid. He of course replies that he will not be killed and that he will become enormously famous in this cattle raid.

She then promises to wait until he is fighting a skilled opponent, who is his equal in all ways, and then she will come to him as an eel in the ford to trip him so that he will be fighting an unfair fight. He replies that he will dash her against a stone to break her ribs and that she won't be healed unless he himself blesses her.

She then promises to come at him as a wolf and tear a strip from his arm during the fighting so that the odds will be really unfair, to which he replies that he will wound her eye with his spear and she won't be healed until he blesses her.

Finally, she says she will appear as a red-eared white heifer driving fifty other cows before her into the ford and the fight will be so unfair that he will be killed and his head taken as a trophy. He pledges to break her leg with a sling stone and that she won't be healed unless he blesses her, which he will not do. The two then go their separate ways.

The Táin Bó Cúailnge

The big cattle raid that the Morrigan predicted in the Tain Bo Regamna has now come to pass. In this part we are going to look only at the actions of the Morrigan in dealing with Cu Chulainn – keep in mind though this is not her only appearances in this story, nor even her most important ones in my opinion.

We begin with the story of King Buan's Daughter, but here's the thing about that: (1) it only appears as far as I know in one recorded version of the Táin Bó Cúailnge, (2) it is basically a modified and condensed version of some of the events in the Táin Bó Regamna which is older, specifically the threats to attack Cu Chulainn; some scholars have suggested this episode was added later by a scribe trying to justify the Morrigan's interaction with Cu Chulainn within the text and (3) I would highly advise taking the events with a huge grain of salt as we know that the Morrigan has previously been deceptive towards Cu Chulainn. I personally don't think the proclamation of love or offer to help him are genuine, but you can decide for yourself.

King Buan's Daughter

Cu Chulainn was guarding the ford after many long days fighting when he saw a beautiful young woman approaching. He asks her who she is and she says that she is the daughter of King Buan, and that she fell in love with him after hearing of his glorious deeds and has brought her treasure and her cows with her. He tells her it's not a good time, and that they are struggling and hungry so he isn't in a good position to meet a woman. She says that she could help him, but he replies *'I am not here for a woman's ass'*.

She then promised to cause him trouble by coming against him when he is fighting, tangling his legs in the form of an eel. Cu Chulainn replies that he prefers that to the King's daughter and says he will break her ribs and she will not be healed unless he blesses her. She then said she will drive cattle at him while in the form of a wolf to which he replies that he will smash her eye with a stone from his sling and she won't be healed unless he blesses her. Finally, she says she will come at him in the form of a hornless red heifer, and he says that he will break her legs with a sling stone and she won't be healed unless he blesses her. Then they part ways.

The Death of Loch

Cu Chulainn found himself fighting against the warrior Loch who was a formidable opponent and while they fought in the river ford the Morrigan came from the sidhe to fulfill her promise to destroy Cu Chulainn. She came in the form of a white red-eared heifer with fifty white cows, each bound to another with a bronze chain. Cu Chulainn threw a stone with his sling and broke one of her eyes.

Then she came at him again, this time in the form of a black eel who twined around his ankles and tripped him, so that he fell and Loch wounded him in the chest. Cu Chulainn rose when he was wounded and smashed the eel against some rocks, breaking its ribs.

Finally, she came at him as a grey-red wolf bitch, driving cows before her, and she bit him and distracted him so that Loch wounded him again this time in the loins. Cu Chulainn cast a spear at her and wounded her a third time, and was so enraged that he cast the Gae Bulga at Loch, impaling him upon it and mortally wounding him. Dying Loch asked that Cu Chulainn grant him the dignity of dying on his face not his back so that everyone would know he had not died trying to run away, which Cu Chulainn did.

Cu Chulainn then composed a poem of the fight in which he recounted the events, and mentions the wolf and eel attacking him, calling the Morrigan 'Badb'.

The Healing of the Morrigan

After fighting Cu Chulainn has what may fairly be called a very bad day, with Medb violating the agreement of fair combat which dictated that warriors would fight one on one by sending six warriors at once against Cu Chulainn.

The Morrigan then appeared again to Cu Chulainn disguised as an old woman[1] who was milking a three-teated cow. Because he had wounded her and no one could be healed from such wounds unless Cu Chulainn blessed them.

Desperately thirsty Cu Chulainn begs the old woman for a drink and she gives him some milk from the first teat. He responds by saying *"May this be a cure for me, O old woman"* and so the Morrigan's eye was healed. He begged for another drink and she gave him milk from the second teat to which he said *"May she be healthy now who gave this"* and her ribs were healed. He begged a third drink and she gave him one from the final teat, after which he said *"blessing of the Gods and un-Gods on you, woman"* at which her leg was healed. And so the Morrigan was healed.

Medb then attacks him again with her warriors and he defeats them.

The Death of Cu Chulainn

Rounding out our modern re-telling of the Morrigan's interactions with Cu Chulainn we have what may be called the fi nal chapter of the Ulster Cycle, the Death of Cu Chulainn. I will say this, there is some disagreement about some of the details here, specifically in some places who was doing what, and there are multiple versions of this story. I am giving a re-telling which I feel is true to the spirit of the originals, but of course I encourage everyone to read the originals themselves.

The cattle raid of Cúailnge was done and over and Cu Chulainn had several other adventures since that time, but he had made some dangerous enemies, one of which was Queen Medb who had never forgiven him for ruining her plans to take the Brown Bull, or for killing so many of her champions. And she probably still remembered that time he killed her pets sitting on her shoulder when he flung a sling stone at her, as well. So Medb had gotten together many warriors who also hated Cu Chulainn, and she had gotten the children of Calatin, a warrior

Cu Chulainn had killed in the Táin Bó Cúailnge to ally with her against him. The daughters of Calatin were fearsome looking, each having only one eye, and Medb sent them to be trained in witchcraft.

Medb began attacking Ulster again with her army and her new champions, hoping to draw Cu Chulainn out to fight. Initially the people who cared about Cu Chulainn tried to trick him into not joining the fighting in several ways, including sending him to a valley where he would be unable to hear any outside noises, but he still saw the smoke rising from the other army and insisted on fighting.

The night before his final battle the Morrigan broke his chariot, trying to prevent his going because she knew he would not return. When he tried to leave the next morning there were several ill omens, including the weapons falling from the racks and Cu Chulainn's own brooch pin falling and cutting his foot. When he called for his chariot to be readied Laeg replied that for the first time his horse, the Grey of Macha was refusing to be harnessed. Cu Chulainn went out himself and spoke to the horse, who turned his left side to his master three times then cried tears of blood at his feet.

All the women wept to see him going, and after he left, he saw a woman [the Morrigan or Badb] washing bloody clothes in a river. When he called to her and asked whose clothes she was washing she responded that it was his own.

Then he came upon the three one-eyed daughters of Calatin disguised as three crones. They were at a cooking hearth by the side of the road cooking a dog on a rowan spit, and Cu Chulainn had geasa on him not to eat at a wild cooking hearth or to eat his namesake so he tried to hurry past. The three witches called out to him though and asked him to join them, and when he refused, they mocked him for turning down their hospitality saying he would have stopped for a grand meal but not for the small bit they had to offer. Since there was also a geis on refusing hospitality Cu Chulainn was literally screwed if he did and screwed if he didn't, so he stopped. One of the women offered him the shoulder of the cooked dog with her left hand and he took it in his left hand and ate, then put the bone beneath his left leg; the arm and leg immediately weakened.

Then he came to the plain of Muirthemne where the warrior Erc has set up an ambush for him, with many warriors waiting. And it had been said that kings would fall by Cu Chulainn's spear so they had devised a clever strategy to get him to give them his spear, that is they set up three pairs of men fighting each other and with each stood a satirist. As Cu Chulainn went across the plain fighting the army he came upon the first pair of fighting men and the satirist called to him to stop them, so he did by killing them. Then the satirist asked for his spear, and when Cu Chulainn refused the satirist said he would make a mockery of him for not giving it so Cu Chulainn hurled his spear through the man. Then his enemies, Lugaid and Erc, recovered it and Lugaid asked the sons of Calatin who would be killed by the spear and one replied that a king would be killed by it. So Lugaid threw it and struck Laeg, who was acclaimed as the king of charioteers. Laeg died and Cu Chulainn carried on, removing the spear and driving his own chariot.

Then he came upon the second pair and again was asked to stop them, again killed them and had the satirist demand his spear. Again, he refused and the satirist said he would mock him but Cu Chulainn said he had already bought his honor that day, so the satirist promised to mock Ulster if he did not so he threw it through the man and this time Erc recovered it. He asked the sons of Calatin who would be killed by the spear and they replied a king so Erc threw it and mortally wounded the Grey of Macha who was called the king of horses. Cu Chulainn pulled the spear out and the Grey of Macha broke free and ran to the Sliab Fuait with half the yoke still attached.

Again, he drove across the plain and this time saw the third pair fighting and again stopped them when requested and as before the third satirist asked for his spear. He refused and the satirist said he would mock him but Cu Chulainn said he had already bought his honor that day, so the satirist promised to mock Ulster if he did not and he said he had paid for that already as well. Finally, the satirist promised to mock his whole people and Cu Chulainn threw the spear butt first through the man. Lugaid recovered it and asked the sons of Calatin who the spear would kill. They said a king, so as Cu Chulainn drove again through the army Lugaid threw the spear, disemboweling the king of Ireland's heroes. His second horse broke its yoke as well and fled, stranding the chariot with Cu Chulainn in it.

Now he asked his enemies if he could go to the nearby lake for a drink and they agreed as long as he promised to come back, and he said he would or if he could not, they would have to come get him. And he held his guts to his chest with his hands and went to get a drink, and wash himself, and prepare for death. On his return to the plain he saw a great pillar stone and he tied himself to it so that he would die on his feet. When his enemies gathered around him, they did not know if he was alive or dead yet, and as they waited the Grey of Macha came back and defended him for as long as he lived.

Finally, the Morrigan and her sisters came in the guise of hooded crows and perched on the pillar, or some say on Cu Chulainn's shoulders, and so his enemies knew that the life was gone from him and they closed in to claim their battle trophies, carrying off his head and right hand to Tara, although Lugaid lost his own right hand when Cu Chulainn's sword fell and severed it.

Cu Chulainn's allies were hurrying to the plain and they met the Grey of Macha on the road, covered in blood and gore, and knew that Cu Chulainn had died. And they followed the horse to his body, where the Grey of Macha stood and laid his head against Cu Chulainn's chest in grief.

End Notes

1 I just want to note the Irish used actually specifies a woman over 70 years old.

Chapter 6

Ancient Goddess in the Modern World

One of the challenges with a deeper understanding of the Morrigan is finding a way to conceptualize her in the modern world and also to relate to some of her purviews in a modern way. What I often see is people trying to force the Morrigan into roles that don't suit her nature rather than trying to understand her nature and how she would organically find a place in modern paganism. In this chapter I want to look at some of the main areas where we find this, including how we understand sovereignty, and the Morrigan as a mother or sex goddess. With all of these I'd like to challenge readers to set aside preconceived notions and contemplate the ideas being presented with an open mind.

The Morrigan and Sovereignty

We talk a lot about goddesses of sovereignty, especially in Irish polytheism, but there is a disconnect between the ancient understanding of what those goddesses did and what they are seen to do in a modern context. Often the way that sovereignty is perceived is heavily colored by modern ideals of the value of the individual and of individual freedom, while the ancient view saw sovereignty as the right of one person to exert control over others. This disconnect is born from a misunderstanding or romanticism of the historic concept and yet may also represent a way in which the old gods are evolving and adapting to a new world.

To begin, sovereignty itself may not be a very good translation of the Old Irish word flaitheas, although it is one given by the dictionary. Flaitheas more properly should probably be translated as "rulership" or the right to rule, which is also another of its meanings. The ancient goddesses of sovereignty gave the kings and chieftains the right to rule over the people, effectively legitimizing their kingship. To have the blessing or approval of the goddess of sovereignty, to symbolically marry her, was to be given the divine right to rule. In the context of ancient Irish culture this was a very important thing because only with the approval of this goddess, only with flaitheas, could a king prosper in his rule; through right relation to the goddess of flaitheas a king could bring abundance and security to his people and land. Angering her though would lead to destruction, one way or another.

Where this gets tricky linguistically is that the word sovereignty in English not only means the authority of someone or something over a group, but also freedom from external control. While the Old Irish word means ruling, and is even used as a word to mean a kingdom or realm, the English word only partially overlaps these meanings and includes connotations of independence and freedom that are entirely lacking in the Irish. In this case the choice of words in translation is very important, especially since the newer understanding has grown largely out of the concepts surrounding the English term, not the Irish.

We live in a world where we are disconnected from the idea of sovereignty, in part because the modern idea is far different from the ancient one. Several Irish goddesses were bestowers of flaitheas, deciding who would rule over the geographic area they were associated with, such as Macha in Armagh or Aine in Limerick. A king or chieftain successfully rule over the land and people of his domain was dependent on the blessing of this goddess. Sometimes the king would ritually marry the goddess to symbolize his union with her, in other cases she would appear and offer him a drink from a cup representing sovereignty. It was very important that the king live in right relation with the goddess of sovereignty because to do so would bless his people with abundance and prosperity, while offending her or angering her would bring about loss and scarcity.

Many people today when they see the word sovereignty used interpret it not as the right to rule a place and its people but rather as a word relating to personal autonomy. This may be inaccurate in a historical context, but for those of us living in a place without a functioning monarchy what else would sovereignty be? When there is no king to marry the land, no chieftain to be chosen and blessed by the goddess, then what becomes of the concept of sovereignty itself? How can we internalize it and make it personal, make it about our right to rule over our own land, which is our body, our own kingdom, which is ourselves. When we honor the goddess of sovereignty in our lives, we are honoring a modern concept of sovereignty, but that is no less impactful or important than the ancient one. It is different, and more personal, but just as powerful in its own way to call on a goddess of sovereignty today as ever.

The Morrigan's most well-known, and arguably main, aspects may be battle, death, and war but she also has other purviews including sovereignty and that is what many of her followers today seem to connect most strongly with. In our modern world many people feel disempowered in their lives, making the idea of reconnecting with personal power an alluring one, and something that the Morrigan can help with by pushing us to find our own sense of sovereignty. She is not, in this case, a giver of sovereignty to those who seek it, but rather she will challenge us to fight for the independence and strength we need to feel like we are in control of our own selves.

Over time the concept of sovereignty has evolved. It is no longer restricted to kings and rulers but has become something personal, something that we all have within us. Whereas the Irish word flaitheas applies very specifically to rulership, kingdoms, and domains, the English translation of sovereignty has different meanings which have come to shape our understanding. Sovereignty is not only about rulership and authority over others, but also about personal autonomy and freedom, in essence about our ability to rule over ourselves. To have personal sovereignty is to stand in our personal power, take responsibility for all of our actions and their consequences, and to embrace the idea that we are ultimately our own authority. Our bodies belong only to ourselves. Our lives are lived as we choose to live them, whether that is for ourselves or for others, for our own happiness, or for other peoples'. Personal sovereignty is a choice, even when we are in situations where we can't control or choose what is happening, we can choose how we react to the situations we are in. We each have the possibility of connecting to the goddess of sovereignty. We each have the potential for self-determination. We each have the capacity to be completely in control of ourselves and our own actions, to live by choice and not by chance, and in doing so to live in right relation to the goddess of sovereignty and earn her blessing in our life.

Just as the word itself has changed with time, so too has the purview of the goddess of sovereignty changed over time. The Morrigan is still who and what she was historically, nothing has fallen away from her, but new things have been added as the world and human society changed, because the gods grow and adapt with us. In the past she might decide who would rule by shaping the outcome of a battle, or by challenging kings to act when action was needed. Macha, a goddess who is one of the three Morrigans, was directly associated with sovereignty by blessing or cursing kings, and, as Macha Mongruadh, with choosing the king. In a modern context the Morrigan comes to us individually and provokes us to embrace our own autonomy, to find our own sense of personal sovereignty.

The Morrigan is not known as a gentle goddess although how she interacts with us can depend on the situation and the person. In inciting us to find our own sovereignty she is challenging.

Like a smith separating the dross from the good material she does what is needed to make us stronger. She pushes us to confront our fears, to admit our weaknesses and turn them into strengths, to face the things we want only to avoid, to confront instead of hide. She teaches us that sovereignty has a price, but if we are willing to pay that price, she will help us become better, stronger people. She does not give anything easily or freely but she will push us to find our own way to our personal power. Because what she offers has great value it is not easily earned nor freely given, but it is more than worth the effort.

The Morrigan does not give sovereignty – she urges us to embrace our own by challenging us to find our strength and stand in our power. We may each have different definitions of what sovereignty is, but however we choose to define it we should strive to understand how it fits into our life. Decide for yourself what sovereignty is and then find a way to embrace it. The Morrigan stands before us and says: *"Who rules your life? Dare to be your own sovereign, dare to rule over your own flesh, dare to be in control of your own self."*

The Morrigan and the Idea of Mother Goddesses

This idea for this section was actually started in a conversation about the Morrigan as a mother goddess and I want to say right at the off that I have nothing against people who believe that she is. Modern worshipers see the Morrigan in diverse ways that are often deeply significant for each individual and I am in no way trying to argue against those views. You can have whatever personal relationship with any deity you feel that you have, and don't worry about whether or not those views are shared. It may not be my view, but such is life – and likewise my views and how I relate to her shouldn't be terribly upsetting to you if they don't agree with your own. Personal views and understandings by their nature will always be deeply personal and individual.

But I think it's important to have this discussion as the idea of the Morrigan as a mother goddess, like the idea of her as a sex goddess, which we will also be discussing, is sometimes taken outside the realm of personal interaction and projected onto her character more generally and that is a bit problematic. Seeing her as a mother figure to yourself is one thing; stating that she is a mother-type deity in a general sense is another.

The Morrigan is not a mother goddess in the modern neopagan sense. I am aware of books who try to fit her into a Maiden-Mother-Crone paradigm will put her, often, into the mother category but she doesn't fit into this by her nature. The idea of a triple M-M-C goddess comes to us from the 20th century, while the kinds of triple deities we find in older Irish mythology are usually sisters and act together or in activities along the same lines. With the Morrigan and her two sisters those lines are war and prophecy, while for another example with Brighid those lines would be creativity and creation (depending on how we are viewing healing).

From a purely mythological standpoint as a mother the evidence for her having children is complicated. She is said to have a son named Meiche – but he had to be killed because he had three serpents in his heart who would have grown and destroyed Ireland. The Lebor Gabala Erenn names her as the mother of a trio of sons, but that may be a case of conflating her with another goddess in an attempt to homogenize the folklore when the stories were written down. She is named as the mother of a daughter by the Dagda, but the daughter is an obscure figure who we don't know much about. She is also said to have 52 children who were warriors in the Silva Gadelica, but in context it seems likely they were actually people dedicated to her and not physical children. So, there's not much solid evidence for her as a physical mother of children and certainly not in the prodigious way of, say, Flidais who one can easily argue does fit the image of a mother goddess.

Secondly from a more Jungian viewpoint she doesn't fit the archetypal pattern of the Mother very well either. The Mother, as an archetype[1], is gentle, nurturing, caring, loving, and supportive, because she represents the idealized qualities of the concept of a mother. The Morrigan is many, many awesome and inspiring things but when I think of words to describe her "nurturing" and "gentle" don't exactly spring immediately to my mind. Not to say she can't be those things if she is in the mood to be – blackthorn can make a safe refuge for small birds avoiding predators, but that doesn't mean my first thought when it's mentioned is "cuddly" (seriously have you seen those thorns?). My point here – no pun intended, mostly – is that while I do think the Morrigan can be caring and supportive to those who honor her, I don't think occasionally acting that way or taking on that role under specific circumstances makes her the embodiment of the Mother in an archetypal way. I do think that it's a very interesting thing that so very many neopagans seem to be seeking out a Mother in the goddesses they honor, to the point of seeing that Mother and the qualities of mothering in goddesses who far more easily could be said to embody the Anti-Mother or Negative Mother.

The Morrigan to me, if I were going to describe her in a personal sense, is a force of incitement and empowerment. She can be supportive, but she also pushes me to achieve. She can be caring, but she doesn't let me slack or give excuses. She can be gentle, but she can also be brutal, harsh, and push me past what I thought was my limit so that I realize that I am stronger and braver than I realized. She can be nurturing, but she nurtures my potential by driving me to achieve and pushing me to excel. She will stand up and defend me only until the moment I can do it for myself, and she will be urging me the entire time to stand up. She does not chase away my nightmares, but teaches me to face them. That is who she is to me.

For myself, my own viewpoint is both simpler and, in a way, more complex. She just doesn't resonate with me as a mother goddess, nor as a deity, quite frankly, of sex, nor of fertility[2] although these are all popular views of her. I don't see her as a goddess of rebirth or birth either – although I'll repeat here that if you do, that's fine, I'm not trying to attack anyone else's opinions, just to share my own thoughts. To me a mother Goddess is about more than fiercely protecting your children or family – after all isn't that what most warriors are doing? Wasn't that why the pleas of Cu Chulainn's father, Súaltaim, during the Táin Bó Cúailnge to arouse the Ulstermen to fight include saying "your wives and sons and children are taken"? I feel like being fiercely protective speaks more to her warrior side than anything else, to the desire and ability to fight for what needs to be fought for. What makes her a goddess of fertility? Being female and connected to sex? So far no one has been able to offer an actual explanation beyond a tenuous argument that as Anu if she's connected to the earth, she is by default a fertility goddess, to which I would ask everyone to consider – what defines a fertility goddess? For me personally a fertility deity is someone I pray to for physical fertility of myself, my animals, and my crops and while I may ask the Morrigan to increase my cattle via successful raiding she just isn't who I would go to for physical fertility (which again isn't to say she might not answer someone for that if she felt like it, she's a goddess she can influence whatever she wants to). No mythic associations, no folklore, so just not something I see as her bailiwick. The same arguments hold true for re-birth and birth.

I'll emphasize again – and again and again – though that just because a deity is generally most strongly associated with something doesn't mean that they are limited to those things. To use a rough analogy, the Morrigan can be a goddess of war, battle, and death but may also choose to relate to an individual in a unique way, just as a person can specialize in a skill but also be able to do other things they have no training in. I think where it starts to get messy is when someone has a personal association with a deity and then associates that outwards into a generalization for everyone. Also, I know some people really dislike the idea of a deity being the "goddess of —" because they find it limiting to that deity, but it's pretty clear looking at both ancient pagan religions and modern ones that deities have always specialized. If you look at Hinduism, Santeria, any tribal religion, Egyptian paganism, Hellenismos, Shinto, and so on some gods were always worshiped for certain things and other gods for other things – the idea of any one deity doing it all is very uncommon. I might even venture to say that the idea of an interactive, all-powerful, all-influential, all-encompassing deity in a polytheistic sense is very post-modern but I'm sure someone will find an example to contradict me.

I'm not always very good at binary thinking, and this is an example of where my perspective varies because I just don't see the Morrigan as defined, in any significant way, by her anatomy. Yes, she's a goddess. Yes, she in many ways exemplifies female empowerment. But I just can't bring myself to see her as defined by those features which people emphasize – her ability to give birth, her ability to have sex, her ability to mother – these are all part of her but only in a modern context have they become aspects which we focus on and emphasize. And in some cases, in some contexts I have seen them emphasized in ways that reduce her to just another overly-sexualized woman in a culture that doesn't respect women very much. I've seen male devotees talk about her as if she was their girlfriend or some sort of anime fantasy, emphasizing only her sex and fertility aspects; and that does make me uncomfortable and more than a bit offended. I've seen female devotees talk about her as if she was nothing but gentle and loving kindness, the perfect mother fulfilling that fantasy for them. And maybe she is those things to those people, because maybe that's what they need, or maybe she isn't and they just see what they want to see, I have no idea, and I honestly can say it's between Her and them. But I just can't see Her in those ways. To me she will always be powerful and awesome – awe inspiring – not because she is female but because she is Herself.

The Morrigan, Sex, and the Idea of a Sex Goddess

Let me repeat that we all see the Gods differently and I know that sometimes a person can relate to a deity in a way that is unusual (comparatively) or unique to them; maybe this is how they need to see that deity for personal reasons. What I want to address here is something that I've seen more and more often among people discussing the Morrigan, and that is the idea that she is a goddess of sex or sexuality – not that an individual relates to her that way but that it is a definitive part of who she, as a deity, is. People even claim that it is one of her main purviews. I've seen it said in many places by many different people, and in a wider way we can see it reflected in the way she is often shown in artwork: scantily clad (or nude), alluringly posed, oozing sex appeal even on a battlefield or among corpses.

I won't address the way she appears in statues here, as that gets into a wider social issue. I will only say that I don't think clothes or lack of clothes is the problem. I love Paul Borda's Morrigan statue, which depicts her nude and as a warrior. I don't find it sexy at all or male gaze oriented and I think that's the key. One can be naked and powerful or one can be naked and vulnerable, and too often the 'nude Morrigan' artwork shows her as the latter. And I'm sorry people but when she's being shown looking like a very young woman who couldn't physically hold the blade she's carrying – or is holding it point down over her own foot! – it's pretty clear that the image isn't meant to depict a powerful goddess but simply an attractive female body. What I want to discuss here is why, exactly, this idea of the Morrigan as a goddess of sexuality and sex is problematic to me and why it concerns me to see it spreading.

One of the most often repeated things I run across is the idea that the Morrigan has lots of lovers among the gods, or her stories are full of sexual trysts with gods and mortals. So, let's start by looking at the Morrigan's mythology and when and how often she has sexual encounters. Don't worry this won't take long.

The Cath Maige Tuired

The Dagda had a house at Glenn Etin in the north. The Dagda was to meet a woman on a day, yearly, about Samain of the battle at Glen Etin. The Unish of Connacht calls by the south. The woman was at the Unish of Corand washing her genitals, one of her two feet by Allod Echae, that is Echumech, by water at the south, her other by Loscondoib, by water at the north. Nine plaits of hair undone upon her head. The Dagda speaks to her and they make a union. Bed of the Married Couple was the name of that place from then. She is the Morrigan, the woman mentioned particularly here. (translation my own)

Táin Bó Cúailnge:

Cú Chulainn saw coming towards him a young woman of surpassing beauty, clad in clothes of many colours.

'Who are you?' asked Cú Chulainn.

'I am the daughter of Búan the king,' said she. 'I have come to you for I fell in love with you on hearing your fame, and I have brought with me my treasures and my cattle.'

*'It is not a good time at which you have come to us, that is,
our condition is ill, we are starving. So, it is not easy for me to
meet a woman while I am in this strife.'*
   'I shall help you in it.'
   'It is not for a woman's body that I have come.'
   *'It will be worse for you', said she, 'when I go against you
as you are fighting your enemies. I shall go in the form of an
eel under your feet in the ford so that you shall fall.'*
   'I prefer that to the king's daughter,' said he.' – Táin Bó
Cúailnge, Recension 1, O Rahilly translation

So, there you go. That's it. In the first example we see the
Morrigan and the Dagda having a pre-arranged meeting at a set
time and place, and it should be noted that the two are likely
married. The reference above notes this when it says the place
they lay together was called 'the Bed of the Married Couple' and
the Morrigan is called the Dagda's wife in other sources like the
Metrical Dindshenchas. In the second example – which please
note does not occur in all version of the Táin Bó Cúailnge –
we see the Morrigan approaching Cu Chulainn disguised as a
young woman and proclaiming her love for him. I am highly
suspicious, as are several scholars, of the genuineness of this
and believe it is most likely a trick to try to get him to abandon
the ford he is guarding. Some scholars have suggested this bit
of narrative was added later by scribes unfamiliar with the Táin
Bó Regamna who needed an explanation for why the Morrigan
then set herself against Cu Chulainn. In any event as you can
see, she never actually offers him sex or tries to seduce him,
although she does off er her love and her goods as what would
have been either a wife or as a mistress.

   In fairness I will add that there is, as far as I'm aware, one
description of Herself appearing naked, from the Cath Magh
Rath:

Bloody over his head, fighting, crying out
A naked hag, swiftly leaping
Over the edges of their armor and shields
She is the grey-haired Morrigu
(translation mine)

In this text the Morrigan is specifically described as grey-haired and a hag, and is leaping over an army about to engage in battle, shrieking. Why then is it repeated so often that the Morrigan is a sexual goddess and has multiple sexual encounters?

At this point I think a lot of it is simply the internet effect, where one website stated it as a fact at some point[3] and now it gets repeated and passed on as fact. The idea appeals to people for different reasons. In my own experience I have found that some men like the idea of the Morrigan as a goddess of sex and as sexual because it allows them to relate to her the way they would to a beautiful human woman. I have seen some women like this idea because they find it sexually empowering for themselves. There is also, of course, the fact that in video games and fiction she's shown as sexual and sex focused, and while those are fiction and entertainment, we can't underestimate the way that does impact how people start to subconsciously relate to the deity.

That all sounds like it could be good, but it concerns me on a couple levels. Firstly, while I do appreciate the desire for women to feel sexually empowered and to look to a goddess as a role model here, reshaping the Morrigan to do it is only reinforcing existing Western ideas of beauty and female power – we focus on the Morrigan as a young beautiful woman who is powerful because she engages in sexual relationships with men on her own terms. That seems great on the surface, sure, but what about seeing her as beautiful as the naked hag? As the redhaired satirist? As a crow or raven? What about seeing her as powerful without a man? Or simply acknowledging her power as a goddess of battle, incitement, prophecy, and sovereignty? Basically, my question is why do we have to make her into something she isn't when she already is beautiful and powerful in a different way?

The other side of that coin, the objectification, is a more complicated problem. It seems to me to rest not on redefining her power but on reducing it by taking a fearsome goddess of several things that are genuinely terrifying for humans and making her into a deity of things humans find pleasant and enjoyable. Instead of a deity of war and death she becomes a goddess of sexual pleasure; instead of a screaming hag above armies she becomes a young girl with come-hither eyes and scanty clothing. And to me that speaks volumes about containing her power by limiting her to ideas and to an image that our culture sees as both safe and inherently disempowered.

Yes, gods evolve and change with their worshippers, but that change in the past was usually organic and a slow process. We live in a world now where a single person can assert something as fact and that assertion, based in nothing but one person's opinion, can then spread quickly and far as fact – and that in my opinion is not how the evolution of gods has ever worked before. When we take a being with history and depth and layers of mythology and detach them from their own stories and personality and make them nothing more than a mirror for our own desires, we aren't engaging with deity anymore, whether we see deity as archetype or as unique individual beings. Perhaps in time there will be a new deity – a new version – of the older goddess created from this milieu of rootless belief. But it will not be the Morrigan of Irish culture, it will be something created from modern beauty standards and sexual mores. And we need to be aware of that and of what that really means.

The Morrigan isn't, in my opinion, a good candidate for a sex deity – but then who is? Well, I think when we look at the Irish pantheon the Dagda as sex god makes a lot of sense. But I also think that all the same cultural reasons why we, collectively, want to force this title into the Morrigan are the same reasons we avoid it for the Dagda. When we make a powerful female figure sexier, we make her safer, particularly when we are using imagery and language that hinges on defining her by roles our society sees as weaker. When we make a male figure more sexually imposing though one of two things happens: its comedic or its frightening. The Dagda is a physically big figure, a warrior, powerful – the idea of his being a sex deity may frighten some people. He is also often mislabeled as an 'all father'[4] deity and envisioned as a kind of red-haired, portly Santa-type and our culture really dislikes seeing that as sexy, we'd much rather find comedy in it.

And that is also something I think we should give some serious thought to.

People are always free to hold their own opinions. I have shared mine here, and my reasoning for why I think and feel as I do. The Morrigan is not a sex goddess for me, or a goddess of sex or sexuality. But she is fierce, and beautiful, and powerful. She is a goddess of personal autonomy and of the sovereignty of kings. She is the land, blood soaked after battle, and the shrieking cry of warriors plunging blade-first into conflict. She is the voice that inspires the downtrodden to rise up and fight for freedom, and the whispers of prophecy foretelling the fate of all. She is awesome in the oldest sense of the word. And that is enough.

Thoughts on the Morrigan, Service, and Diversity

I want to end this chapter with some thoughts on the value of diversity in the community of modern Morrigan worshippers.

I think it's important to always remember that no single approach will work for everyone. Also, something we all should give more thought to, not only in the general sense that each tradition won't be right for everyone – Gods know recon isn't for everyone – but also that even those who are dedicated to the same deity will find different expressions of that dedication. We each have our own niches within our service. Perhaps we can say that there are often themes within the things people who share a deity are drawn to, commonalities, but each of us finds our own expression. We are each filled with a different passion. It's easy to forget though that those who honor the same deity we honor do not necessarily share the calling that drives us.

I have only rarely met other people dedicated to Macha, but I know many more generally dedicated to the Morrigan. I see the expression of the things that drive them and sometimes I nod in agreement and sometimes I shake my head or shrug. The things that they are so profoundly driven by may or may not be things that I understand or share. In the same way the things that drive me are not the things that drive them. I know many honorable Morrigan's people who have taken up wonderful causes in Her name, including things like raising money to donate to charities like the Wounded Warrior Project. I admire that, but it is not my cause to carry forward.

I have a deep concern for the welfare of children, especially infants and for the rights of parents to provide care. I'm a pretty outspoken against circumcision and strongly advocate breastfeeding rights[5], for example. In fact, the only social protest I've participated in was a "nurse-in" that came about after a woman was asked to stop nursing at a local restaurant. I have helped with fundraisers in my area to donate to the local women's shelter and to food pantries. I don't tie those things directly into my dedication to Macha, but I certainly have come to feel over the years that She is a deity who is very much about justice for women and children[6]. When I think of serving Macha, I can't help but think as well of speaking up in defense of the helpless, especially children, and of defending mother's rights. I feel like that's part of my personal calling. But I have to remind myself that just because these things matter to me doesn't mean they matter to others, not even other people who serve Her. It would be unfair of me to judge others for not sharing in the drive I feel to fight for these things. Instead, I try to see and appreciate the things they do want to fight for.

Some of us are called to write and teach while others sing, or dance, or live quiet lives of devotion. Some of us feel very passionate about a cause, others don't. We are a diverse group, a wide array of people from different walks of life and places – in every sense – who all seek to honor the Morrigan. As tempting as it can be to want to measure everyone by our own standard, we need to let go of the idea of expecting everybody to be like us, to share our goals and ideals. Our service takes many different forms, and we should strive to appreciate the service offered by others, as much as we work at doing the best on our own path.

End Notes

1   A Jungian archetype that is – the word gets tossed around a lot in neopaganism but I honestly don't understand how it's being used about half the time. In Jungian psychology as I understand it, an archetype is an unconscious, inherited idea of the ideal pattern or type of a thing that humans get form the collective unconscious and which is shared across cultures. So hence the archetypal Hero, Mother, and Trickster. Archetypes aren't decided by individuals but are dictated by the sum total of human experience and cultural inheritance.

2   Macha, however, is arguably a fertility goddess something I discuss in my article "Macha, Horses, and Sovereignty" which can be found in the 2015 anthology "Grey Mare on the Hill".

3   This is exactly how the idea that falcons are connected to her and that she is a goddess of rebirth happened. One website more than a decade ago, run by someone who was very honest

that they were posting channeled and personal material said it, and it spread from there. Once it was accepted into the common belief no one really knew where it had come from or why they believed it.

4 Ollathair doesn't mean all father but great or ample father. It certainly connects him to abundance but not to physical proliferation.

5 Every woman must feed her child in the way that is best for them, and I do not judge what way that is, but I am a strong proponent for the right of anyone to feed a child anywhere at any time, and in the support of a person's legal rights to nurse uncovered in public.

6 This has grown out of my contemplation of her cursing the men of Ulster, although I do realize that story has a lot of other layers as well.

Chapter 7

Ways to Feel More Connected

One question that I am asked on a fairly regular basis is what should people who are interested in connecting spiritually to the Morrigan or who are just beginning to honor Her do? I wanted to end this book by looking at this topic, although keep in mind that these are only my ideas and what I have found works well for me. I tend to be a very sensory person so you'll note a lot of this involves sensory experiences – sound, sight, touch – and that may appeal to some people and not to others. These suggestions are meant to be tailored to you personally, so please take them and play with them to find what works best for yourself.

Myths and Stories

The very first thing I'll suggest is to read as many of the old myths and stories as you can, preferably as close to the originals as possible. The re-tellings are nice – obviously I've included some of my own in this book – but many like Lady Gregory's *Gods and Fighting Men* take liberties with the stories and change details that make big differences. This is something you need to be aware of when weighing the value of a source.

I'm always going to be an advocate for going to the source material itself. You can find many of the older stories at Mary Jones *Celtic Literature Collective* and the stories which feature the Morrigan include the Cath Mag Tuired Cunga, Cath Maige Tuired, Lebor Gabala Erenn, and many of the tales in the Ulster Cycle.

Beyond that there are several modern authors who have written in detail about the Morrigan that are worth reading – my favorite is Angelique Gulermovich Epstein's *War Goddess: The Morrigan and Her Germano-Celtic Counterparts.*

Locations

If possible, you should go and visit the places the stories happen in. Smell the air, touch the earth, feel the wind. Stand in the places that the Morrigan herself is said to have stood in, is still said to stand in, like Uaimh na gCat, and feel her presence there. Below I'm going to list a selection of the more well-known or easily accessible sites you may consider, but understand these are not the only possibilities. The Morrigan has many different sites associated with her.

The River Unshin

The river Unshin is the place where it's said, at a ford of this river near Samhain time, the Dagda had a yearly arrangement to meet the Morrigan. He found her straddling the water washing herself with her hair unbound from nine plaits and the two united. Afterwards the place was called 'Lige ina Lanomhnou' which means roughly 'Bed of the Married Couple'. This river is a real place and can be found in Ireland although the exact location of the ford is debated.

Dumha na nGiall

It was then that Badb and Macha and Morrigan went to the Knoll of the Taking of the Hostages, and to the Hill of Summoning of Hosts at Tara, and sent forth magic showers of sorcery and compact clouds of mist and a furious rain of fire, with a downpour of red blood from the air on the warriors' heads; and they allowed the Fir Bolg neither rest nor stay for three days and nights.

– Cet-Chath Maige Tuired

Dumha na nGiall [mound of hostages] is a 5,000-year-old passage tomb at Teamhair [Tara] at the edge of the section known as Raith na Ríg [fort of kings]. The mound is built in the same way as most other passage tombs and includes some beautiful, intricate carving of the stones at the entrance. The mound was actively used for burials for a thousand years and had up to 500 cremated remains in it. The entrance is now blocked with a heavy iron grate but you can still look inside somewhat. This is the location mentioned in the above quote, where the Morrigan, Badb, and Macha went and worked magic against the Fir Bolg when the Tuatha De Danann had first come to Ireland.

Bru na Boinne

There are multiple locations of importance in the Bru na Boinne complex, but of note here is a reference to the 'Bed of the Couple' in the Dindshenchas Bru na Boinde I:

> *Here slept a married pair*
> *after the battle of Mag Tuired yonder,*
> *the great lady and the swart Dagda:*
> *not obscure is their dwelling there.*

It's unclear exactly where this location is within the Neolithic complex although this line from Bru na Boinde II gives us a hint:

> *Behold the Bed of the red Dagda:*
> *on the slope, without rough rigour*

This description comes immediately after one of Sidhe in Broga [Newgrange] and before one of Dá Chích na Morrígna which may also give us a hint of the location we are looking for.

Dá Chích na Morrígna

The Paps of the Morrigan are a pair of hills near the Bru na Boinne complex. They can be seen from Sidhe in Broga [Newgrange].

Cloch an Fhir Mhóir

And there [Cu Chulainn] drank his drink, and washed himself, and came forth to die, calling on his foes to come to meet him.

Now a great mearing went westwards from the loch and his eye lit upon it, and he went to a pillar-stone which is in the plain, and he put his breast-girdle round it that he might not die seated nor lying down, but that he might die standing up. Aided Conculaind

Folklore and local tradition say that Cloch an Fhir Mhóir was the place that Cu Chulainn died at. The standing stone is located in the middle of a private fi eld so if you do try to visit it keep in mind that the fi eld is in active use for farming and be respectful. The stone itself is worth a visit as the location where Cu Chulainn died and therefore where the Morrigan perched either on the pillar itself or on his shoulder.

Uaimh na gCat

Uaimh na gCat, the Cave of Cats, the Cave of the Morrigan and in the Dindshenchas of Odras it is called the sidhe of Cruachan. Also called "Ireland's Hellmouth" by some. To me, after going in and coming back out again, it will always be the Sí of Cruachan but that's another story.

The cave itself, deep down and a slippery climb into the earth to reach, is a natural feature but the entrance is a man-made souterrain which makes for an odd contrast of experience going in and coming out. You ease into the earth, reaching up to touch the Ogham carved on the lintel, and the first dozen feet in is all hard lines and sharp edges – it feels man made. It feels carved. And then that transition point and you leave behind the hand of man and move into the sections made by nature, and it just feels different. Smoother, even where its jagged. Everything here is all wet clay that sucks and clings, as if the cave means to keep you. And maybe it does. But you go anyway, into the darkness that only the deep earth can have, where sunlight has never even been a dream. And maybe you understand why people describe caves as wombs, or maybe you understand why darkness drives some people mad or terrifies them, or maybe down there you find Herself waiting. And that's the cave.

If it's not possible to physically visit these places then quiet meditation wherever you are is good, but I am I do encourage people if it's possible to go to Ireland and visit the sites firsthand. Even if it's a once in a lifetime goal there is a difference between reading about places and actually experiencing them. Until then, of course, you can do your best to feel connected to the locations of the myths, to the places where the Gods are invested in the land itself by learning as much as possible about them. And if it's not possible at all for whatever reason then pictures, videos, or meditation are viable alternatives.

Shrines

Set up a small shrine to her. I'm a fan of statues and artwork and there is a huge amount to choose from for the Morrigan. My favorite statue is Dryad Design's Morrigan, which I bought and then painted myself. There are also a variety of great art prints out there. Beyond that personalize as you see fi t. I like shrines because they provide a quiet place to sit and visually reflect on the Gods, as well as being a place to light candles, burn incense, and make offerings.

Offerings

Speaking of making offerings. A good way to establish a connection to any deity is to begin making offerings to them. For the Morrigan my own preferences are milk (or cream), whiskey, or bread, although I often off er different things spontaneously as well if I feel drawn to.

Prayer

This tends to be less popular with some people but it really is a good way to connect. Whatever works best for you, whether that's formal memorized prayers or spontaneous speaking from the heart, the point is just to reach out and speak to the Gods.

Playlist

I also encourage people to make their own custom playlist of music about the Morrigan or of songs that remind you of her. There are a surprising number of songs about the Morrigan these days that you can check out on YouTube and also a wider array of music that may make you think of her even she's not the intended theme. I really love music as a vehicle for altered states, trancework, and just plain feeling more strongly connected to something. When it comes to the Morrigan my personal favorites are Omnia's 'Morrigan', Darkest Era's 'The Morrigan', Heather Dale's 'The Morrigan', and Cruachan's 'Brown Bull of Cooley' and 'The Morrigan's Call'. I've found that it's really helpful for me in feeling more connected to her to have this sort of resource and it's something that you can truly personalize however you like it.

Jewelry

My final suggestion would be to get a piece of jewelry that represents or symbolizes the Morrigan for you, that you can wear to help you feel more connected to her. This is largely a psychological thing for the person, a physical token to touch when you need that tactile reminder. Over time though it can become sacred in its own right as its blessed or empowered.

There you go, a short basic list but one that I find effective. Many or most of these may just be common sense but I have found they are all helpful, especially if done regularly. Having a regular spiritual practice is vital in my opinion and this is how I incorporate the Morrigan into that.

Conclusion

We began with a poem written from a dream. Let us end together with an experience, shared in what could be used as a guided meditation.

Uaimh na gCat

The entrance is in a field, beneath a hawthorn. It is an unassuming opening into the earth, but there is something intimidating about it. The darkness beyond the stone and grass is deep and full. It invites you in at the same time that it warns you away. But this is why you have come to this place, seeking this cave, seeking this darkness, and you won't be deterred now.

You move into the liminal space of the entrance, pausing and turning to look back at the light you are leaving behind. Above you there is a stone lintel, carved with ogham. Looking up your eyes trace the lines, the stone clear even in the dim light. Then, resolved, you turn away from the world above and begin descending into a different world.

The stone path is not easy but clearly bears the marks of human hands. At first. Your feet feel for steps carved into the passageway, your hands sliding along the walls. The darkness around you is so complete and solid it fills you and becomes part of your existence. It is a living thing, coiling around you, pulling you deeper.

In this place you can't rely on sight so your other senses lead you. You touch the walls and feel with your feet. You smell the fullness of the air. You taste moisture and earth on your tongue as you breath. You hear your own movements but also the dripping of water, and the stillness which is its own sound.

Everything is damp and slick and there is a sense of subtle peril. As you move downwards the man-made steps give way to rough rock and you feel the pattern of the path changing beneath your feet, even through thick soled boots. The darkness is different here, thicker, heavier, alive.

The downward journey levels out and you are walking flat now, the space expanding out around you as you enter the cave itself. It is cool here, and damp; the walls are wet and the air you breath in feels like some greater being's exhalation. The floor is inches of clay mud that grab at you and try to hold you in place, making every step forward a battle. Nonetheless you move forward, crossing the main section of the cave until you reach the far side where it begins to climb again before leveling off and disappearing into stone. The mud is like a living thing, moving with you, around you, on you.

You are still now, hands and legs muddy, leaning into the stone wall, feeling the darkness as it encompasses you. It has its own pulse, its own rhythm, and standing there you become part of it, enveloped by it. There is a voice in that darkness that speaks to you, and you listen.

You listen.

When you finally re-emerge into the world above you are not the same.

Appendix A

Online Morrigan Resources

I want to offer personal recommendations for online accessible resources for the Morrigan, to further help people looking for more material. None of these are necessarily blanket endorsements but these are resources that can be found online, are free, and are worth reading. As with anything else in life remember to use critical thinking and to keep in mind that on this subject there can be a variety of opinions.

Dissertations and Papers – There are some great academic works out there on the Morrigan worth checking out. There are also some that I don't entirely agree with but still recommend because they add important layers to any discussion about this complex deity/deities.

- *War-goddesses, furies and scald crows: The use of the word badb in early Irish literature* by Kim Heijda.
- *The 'Mast' of Macha: The Celtic Irish and the War Goddess of Ireland* by Catherine Mowat.
- *War Goddess: The Morrigan and Her Germano-Celtic Counterparts* by Angelique Gulermovich Epstein.
- *Demonology, allegory and translation: the Furies and the Morrigan* by Michael Clarke.
- *The 'Terror of the Night' and the Morrígain: Shifting Faces of the Supernatural* by Jacqueline Borsje.

Blogs – There are a lot of people who blog about the Morrigan these days and I will admit my own suggestions will be limited to people I know, and read regularly. I don't go out looking around for new Morrigan bloggers because I just don't have time. You'll also note this only includes written blogs, which isn't an intentional snub to vloggers or youtubers just a reflection that I hardly ever have time to watch videos on my pc so I can't recommend them.

- Dark Goddess Musings – the blog of author Stephanie Woodfield. Not updated regularly, but has interesting content http://darkgoddessmusings.blogspot.com/
- Lora O'Brien – Author and Freelance Writer – what it says on the tin. Not Morrigan specific but there are Morrigan posts to be found and Lora's writing is always good and worth reading. Lora also offers paid courses on the Morrigan and several other related topics that I highly recommend. https://loraobrien.ie/blog/
- Under the Ancient Oaks – the blog of Druid and author John Beckett. Not Morrigan exclusive either, but she is a frequent topic. https://www.patheos.com/blogs/johnbeckett/2017/07/hear-call-morrigan.html

Websites – An assortment of Morrigan related websites out there that I am aware of and whose content is generally reliable.

- Scath na Feannoige – Morrigan content and content focused on the warrior path. Some free and some paid access, but excellent material. http://www.dunsgathan.net/feannog/index.htm
- Mary Jones Celtic Literature Collective – as advertised, a resource for all things Celtic. Your best source for myths on the Morrigan (in the Irish lit section) and also offering an encyclopedia section http://www.ancienttexts.org/library/celtic/ctexts/index_irish.html
- Story Archaeology – a great resource for newer translations of the myths and discussion of the stories in

context. If you search the site/podcast you'll find multiple results relating to the Morrigan http://storyarchaeology. com/tag/the-morrigan/

- Coru Cathubodua – a site by a group dedicated to the Morrigan, with articles and a resource list http://www. corupriesthood.com/the-morrigan/

Artwork – Some of my personal favorite sources for Morrigan artwork I like. Artwork is, of course, very personal so you may or may not like my suggestions, but either way I encourage you to seek out Morrigan art that speaks to you. I can't list Morrigan resources without including some art, but of course these aren't free.

- The Ever Living Ones, art of Jane Brideson: http:// theeverlivingones.blogspot.com/p/gallery-of-goddesses. html
- Ashley Bryner: https://www.etsy.com/listing/114345068/ phantom-queen?ref=shop_home_active_3
- Gemma Zoe Jones: http://www.gemmazoejones.com/ gallery/2016/11/25/the-morrigan
- Emily Brunner: https://www.emilybrunner.com/store/ morrigan-13
- Valerie Herron: http://www.valerieherron.com/ illustrations.html
- Dryad Design – statuary and jewelry by Paul Borda: https://dryaddesign.com/small-morrigan-statue/

Books – I should probably mention here that generally I am not aware of any decent books on the Morrigan, specifically, that are available *free* online. You can access some older public domain works including Hennessey's *War Goddess* on Sacred Texts but books that old have issues with some seriously outdated scholarship and need to be read with a large grain of salt. They are worth reading with some critical thinking and discernment but I wouldn't give them a blanket recommendation.

Bibliography

Banshenchus, (n.d.)

Carey, J., (2014) A London Library, An Irish Manuscript, A British Myth? The Wanderings of 'The Battle of Moytirra'

Dunn, J., (1914) Tain Bo Cualgne

Gray, E., (1983) Cath Maige Tuired

Green, M., (1992). Animals in Celtic Life and Myth

Gulermovich Epstein, A., (1998). War Goddess: The Morrígan and her Germano-Celtic Counterparts. Electronic version, #148, September, (1998). Retrieved from http://web.archive.org/web/20010616084231/members.loop.com/~musofire/diss/

Gwynne, E., (1906) Metrical Dindshenchas

Heijda, K., (2007). War-Goddesses, Furies, and Scald Crows: the use of the word badb in early Irish literature

Jones, H., (1997) Concerning the Names Morgan, Morgana, Morgaine, Muirghein, Morrigan and the Like. Retrieved from https://medievalscotland.org/problem/names/morgan.shtml

Kelly, F., (2005). A Guide to Early Irish Law

Macalister, R., (1940). Lebor Gabala Erenn

MacCana, P., (1992) Laíded, Gressacht 'Formalized Incitement'

MacKillop, J., (2006) Dictionary of Celtic Mythology

Martin, W., (1895). Pagan Ireland an Archaeological Sketch

Morgan la Fay (2018) The Camelot Project; University of Rochester. Retrieved from http://www.kingarthursknights.com/others/morganlefay.asp

O Donaill, N., (1977). Focloir Gaeilge-Bearla

O hOgain, D., (1991). Myth, Legend, and Romance

— (2006) The Lore of Ireland

O'Mulconry's Glossary (n.d.) http://www.asnc.cam.ac.uk/irishglossaries/

Ó Néill, J., (2003). Lapidibus in igne calefactis coquebatur: The Historical Burnt Mound ‹Tradition›

O Tuathail, S., (1993). The Excellence of Ancient word: Druid Rhetoric from Ancient Irish Tales

Royal Irish Academy (1870). Proceedings of the Royal Irish Academy

Sanas Cormaic (n.d.) http://www.asnc.cam.ac.uk/irishglossaries/

Stokes, W., (1891). Cath Maige Tuired

Windisch, E., (1905). Táin Bó Cúailnge

Readers of ebooks can buy or view any of these bestsellers by clicking on the live link in the title. Most titles are published in paperback and as an ebook. Paperbacks are available in traditional bookshops. Both print and ebook formats are available online.

Find more titles and sign up to our readers' newsletter www.collectiveinkbooks.com/paganism

For video content, author interviews and more, please subscribe to our YouTube channel.

MoonBooksPublishing

Follow us on social media for book news, promotions and more:

Facebook: Moon Books

Instagram: @MoonBooksCI

X: @MoonBooksCI

TikTok: @MoonBooksCI